# Legacy of Action

## How Dr. Geneva Gay
## Transformed Teaching

*Edited by*
La Vonne I. Neal, Ph.D.
Sarah Militz-Frielink, Ph.D.
María T. Colompos-Tohtsonie, Ph.D.
Regina A. Lewis, Ph.D.
Alicia L. Moore, Ph.D.

Apprentice House
Loyola University Maryland
Baltimore, Maryland

First Edition

Printed in the United States of America

Paperback ISBN: 978-1-62720-110-0
E-book ISBN: 978-1-62720-111-7

Cover design: Michael Schwartz/Halodezign LLC
Interior design by: Katie McDonnell
Published by Apprentice House Press

Apprentice House
Loyola University Maryland
4501 N. Charles Street
Baltimore, MD 21210
410.617.5265 • 410.617.2198 (fax)
www.ApprenticeHouse.com
info@ApprenticeHouse.com

Founded in October 2020 on the campus of Loyola University Maryland, the Karson Institute for Race, Peace & Social Justice provides a scholarly space for professors, students, social justice workers, and activists to come together to research, discuss, debate, and explore answers to America's most urgent questions on inequality, injustice, and racial inequity. We are committed to establishing a research and data-based environment built on intersectional liberated ideas and ideologies. We understand that we are a nation of storytellers with a narrative quilt connecting our lives, shared pain, and struggles. As a nation, we are stronger together, but decades of racial injustice, social inequity, and systemic acts of violence against the Black and Brown community have separated us. Throughout history, there have been moments of awakening where we have taken up these broader questions and attempted to settle them. However, we have found that moments can only lead to movements when infrastructure is in place to support operationalizing the work. We are in the midst of one of those moments, and The Institute will be a place to house the research, train our students, and operationalize the movement for racial and social justice. We aim to tell the stories that led us to this moment and capture the stories currently being told. Some of these stories are not new; indeed, America has a long and complicated history of wrestling with the questions of racism and white supremacy. As an institution, Loyola has long been committed to addressing these difficult questions and providing opportunities to implement solutions. As an Institute, the Karson seeks to answer this call and work toward finding solutions.

The Karson Institute currently houses three Centers:

- The Center for Research and Culture (CRC) comprises research fellows and graduate and undergraduate students who conduct and support empirical research on issues at the intersection of race, social justice, peace, education, and advocacy movements in the United States.

- The Center for Public Engagement (CPE) provides a conversational space to discuss relevant and timely racial, social, and healing justice issues and offers regular dialogue sessions.

- The Center for Teaching and Learning (CTL) works to help K-12 educators and administrators throughout the United States excel in their teaching, enhance the culture of teaching, and, in turn, increase the sociocultural perspectives of education.

Through the CRC, the Karson partnered with The Apprentice House to release research books exploring culturally responsive teaching and pedagogy, African American Studies, and cultural studies. Letters of interest may be sent to karsoninstitute@loyola.edu.

Karsonya Wise Whitehead, Ph.D.
*Founding executive director*
The Karson Institute for Race, Peace & Social Justice
Professor, Communication and African and African American Studies
Loyola University Maryland

# CONTENTS

# Contributor Biographies

• **Emily Alicia Affolter, Ph.D.** (she/ella/they) serves as the director of Prescott College's Sustainability Education Ph.D. Program and oversees its Master of Arts in Interdisciplinary Studies. She earned her Ph.D. in Curriculum and Instruction with a focus on Multicultural Education from the University of Washington guided by Dr. Geneva Gay. Dr. Affolter's current scholarship, idea dissemination, and facilitation highlight culturally responsive, decolonial, and sustaining pedagogies for teachers, faculty, and leaders in K-16 settings and STEM higher education.

• **Marisol Alonzo** is a doctoral fellow at the Karson Institute for Race, Peace, and Social Justice at Loyola University Maryland. She created the equity audit to review the equity and inclusion initiatives already undertaken at city neighborhoods, including curricula, instruction, correction, and daily interactions between colleagues. Ms. Alonzo is also the Financial Conflict of Interest Administrator at Texas Tech University's Office of Research and Innovation.

• **Karina Avila** currently serves as a Service Coordinator II in Illinois, helping people with disabilities access choices for a better life. Previously, Karina Avila served as an Adjutant General Corps Captain in the U.S Army. Ms. Avila is a proud mother, advocate for people with disabilities, Latina, and scholar. She is a national book award recipient for *Borders, Bras and Battles: A Practical Guide to Mentor Undergraduate Women to Achieve Career Success.*

• **Courtney Carroll** is the Strategic Communications Analyst for the Karson Institute for Race, Peace and Social Justice. She earned a Bachelor of Arts degree at Loyola University Maryland in Communications with a specialization in Advertising and Public Relations. She has consulted with the National Women's Studies Association (NWSA) for several months and has recently been promoted to Special Projects Manager for the NWSA.

- **María Colompos-Tohtsonie, Ph.D.**, has a doctorate in Educational Leadership and Policy from Texas Tech University. She is a national book award recipient for *Borders, Bras and Battles: A Practical Guide to Mentor Undergraduate Women to Achieve Career Success*. Dr. Colompos-Tohtsonie's research and publications include mentoring students who are culturally and/or linguistically diverse, education policy, historical and contemporary legal procedures, culturally-responsive leadership, and public policy.

- **Kelly J. Cross, Ph.D.** (she/they), Assistant Professor in the Wallace H. Coulter Department of Biomedical Engineering (BME) at Georgia Tech and Emory University, is a data-informed, transformational, mission-focused culturally responsive practitioner, researcher, and educational leader. Dr. Cross was the lead editor of the book, Queering the STEM Culture in US Higher Education, and her complimentary professional activities promote inclusive excellence through collaboration. She is an NSF CAREER awardee, delivered multiple distinguished lectures, and has received a national mentoring award

- **Joseph Flynn, Ph.D.**, is the Executive Director for Equity and Inclusion and Associate Professor of Curriculum and Instruction at Northern Illinois University. In addition to his professional development work around culture and equity, he is the founder of the Social Justice Summer Camp for Educators, held annually at Northern Illinois University. He is also author of *White Fatigue: Rethinking Resistance for Social Justice* (Peter Lang, 2018).

- **Erika L. Freitas, Ph.D.**, is the Assistant Dean for Equity, Diversity, and Inclusion at the University of Colorado Skaggs School of Pharmacy and Pharmaceutical Sciences. She is a certified Anti-Defamation League trainer and a diversity consultant with extensive experience in designing, developing, and implementing culturally responsive approaches to educating healthcare professionals, anti-bias and bullying prevention school-wide programs, workshops for students of all ages, and professional development sessions for educators, counselors, and administrators.

• **Regina Lewis, Ph.D.,** is Professor Emerita and Communication Department Chair (RET.) at Pikes Peak State College. She is a United States Air Force War Veteran and a nationally recognized keynote speaker and facilitator in the areas of culturally responsive teaching, interpersonal and intercultural communication, and organizational leadership. Additionally, Dr. Lewis specializes in cross-cultural leveraging, executive coaching, and policy analytics.

• **Alicia Moore, Ph.D.,** is a Cargill Endowed Associate Professor and Education Department Chair at Southwestern University in Georgetown, Texas. She is an Educational Consultant whose expertise and research interests include: Special Education, Early Childhood, Culturally Responsive Pedagogy, the Experiences of Preservice Teachers, Diversity, Belonging, Inclusion, and Equity in Higher Education. She is the Co-Editor of the Black History Bulletin published by the Association for the Study of African American History (ASALH).

• **Sarah Militz-Frielink, Ph.D.,** teaches classes at the Center for Black Studies and the College of Education at Northern Illinois University. Dr. Militz-Frielink has presented on culturally responsive teaching at the Association for the Study of African American Life and History's Annual National Carter G. Woodson workshop. She is the author and co-author of three books including *Liberation in Higher Education: A White Researcher's Journey through the Shadows* (Peter Lang, 2019).

• **La Vonne I. Neal, Ph.D.,** is Professor Emerita and Associate Vice President (RET.) in Administration and Finance at Northern Illinois University. Dr. Neal is a teacher--educator whose work in the design and implementation of culturally responsive teaching methods has earned wide recognition both among educators and in the popular press. For example, her research on the correlation between African American male students' walking styles and their placement in special education courses has been featured globally in mass media. Neal is a national book award recipient for *Borders, Bras and Battles: A Practical Guide to Mentor Undergraduate Women to Achieve Career Success.*

• **Tierra Parsons** is a native of Taylorsville, North Carolina and a well-being and psychology and social work advocate. She is a doctoral student at the University of North Carolina at Charlotte, and has 18 years of experience working with individuals from diverse backgrounds in the areas of mental wellness, social justice, community engagement, and higher education. Her research interest focuses on the well-being and affirmation of girls of color in urban schools and communities.

• **Kim Pearson** is a Professor of journalism and professional writing at The College of New Jersey, a journalist who has been published in the Online Journalism Review, Black Enterprise, and Newsday, among other outlets, and a civic media researcher whose research on improving science literacy and civic engagement has garnered support from the National Science Foundation, Microsoft Research, and the New Jersey Council of the Humanities. Pearson's professional affiliations include the Online News Association, the Society of Environmental Journalists, the Association for the Study of African American Life and History, Phi Kappa Phi and the National Association of Black Journalists.

• **Annette Teasdell, Ph.D.,** is an Assistant Professor of Curriculum and Instruction and Coordinator of the Special Education Program at Clark Atlanta University. With over 15 years of teaching at the post-secondary and secondary levels, she grounds her research in the fundamental belief that culturally responsive pedagogy and a corrected curriculum can disrupt miseducation and improve student outcomes. Dr. Teasdell's research has been published in several peer-reviewed journals and she is the co-author of the book *Race, Class, Gender, and Immigrant Identities in Education: Insights and Perspectives from First and Second Generation Ethiopian Students*, which is published by Palgrave MacMillan.

• **Shanell Walter, Captain (CPT U.S. Army)**, is an academic and military science scholar. CPT Walter is currently assigned as the Essential Personnel Services Officer in Charge (OIC) for the 82$^{nd}$ Airborne Division, providing human resources support to more than 17,000 paratroopers. CPT Walter's personal awards and decorations include The Meritorious Service Medal, The Army Commendation Medal with Combat Device, The Army Commendation Medal (with 2 Oak Leaf Clusters), Afghanistan Campaign Medal, NATO Medal., National Defense Service Medal, and Army Service Ribbon. Additionally, she is a national book award recipient for *Borders, Bras and Battles: A Practical Guide to Mentor Undergraduate Women to Achieve Career Success.*

• **Greg Wiggan, Ph.D.,** is Professor of Urban Education, Adjunct Professor of Sociology, and affiliate faculty member of Africana Studies at the University of North Carolina at Charlotte. His research addresses school effects that promote high achievement in urban and other minoritized students. He has completed more than 100 publications, inclusive of over 30 education books, which appears in more than 70 countries and over 6,000 college and university libraries (WorldCat, 2022).

• Karsonya Wise Whitehead, Ph.D., is the founding director of The Karson Institute for Race, Peace & Social Justice and a professor of communication and African and African American Studies at Loyola University Maryland. She is the author of five books, including *Notes from a Colored Girl: The Civil War Pocket Diaries of Emilie Frances Davis*, which received both the 2015 Darlene Clark Hine Book Award from the Organization of American Historians and the 2014 Letitia Woods Brown Book Award from the Association of Black Women Historians; *Letters to My Black Sons: Raising Boys in a Post-Racial America*; and the forthcoming *my mother's tongue: dispatches from baltimore's black butterfly.*

# PREFACE

## Echoes of Geneva Gay's Words: "Culturally Responsive Teaching, Gives Meaning to Diversity Without Hierarchy"

*By La Vonne I. Neal*

The purpose of this volume—*Legacy of Action: How Dr. Geneva Gay Transformed Teaching*, is to share how the echoes of Gay's words have traveled across generations, continents, disciplines, professions, and continue to motivate and inspire. Our book begins with this brief preface followed by an introduction and 10 essays situated within four thematic sections. Throughout the essays, authors reminisce about how Gay's words, reverberated in their undergraduate and/or graduate classes, academic conferences, and professional development workshops, helped them shape their scholar identities, professional careers, and impact their respective professions and communities.

So, what is the origin story of this textual gathering, this volume? My fellow contributors and I are a community that is culturally, linguistically, and/or ethnically diverse. What connects us is multicultural education, a field of study and research that supports all students' learning experiences to inspire them to achieve beyond measure. One of Gay's many contributions to multicultural education is her theory—"Culturally Responsive Teaching." For over a decade, many of us have met each year across professional spaces and Gay's words continue to echo throughout the halls of a particular conference—the ASALH Conference (The Association for the Study of African American Life and History). Yes, that is one of our multicultural education homes regardless of our disciplines. Dr. Carter G. Woodson a harbinger of multiculturalism, established ASALH in 1915 and the communal energy there helps us keep our souls intact, it is "easy like Sunday morning." Each year, many of us facilitate the ASALH Teacher Workshop that is held during the ASALH conference. While speaking at one of the ASALH Teacher Workshops, Gay provided us with the purest descriptor of culturally responsive teaching—"culturally responsive teaching, gives meaning to diversity without hierarchy."

I conclude with this thought that brings me joy—every Autumn, following the echoes of Geneva Gay, we, this diverse community make our sojourn to ASALH without hierarchy.

# INTRODUCTION

# Celebrating and Extending Dr. Geneva Gay's Educational Thought

*By María T. Colompos-Tohtsonie*

Dr. Geneva Gay once said, "Intention without action is insufficient." In this book, we feature a series of authors from diverse disciplinary locations who both celebrate and extend the culturally responsive teaching framework[1] developed by the internationally-renowned educational theorist, Geneva Gay that has inspired action. Gay's scholarly innovations have been remarkably consequential by any measure, and as the pages ahead will demonstrate, her intellectual, moral, and personal influence on generations of educators has already proven to be powerful and enduring. Gay's theoretical development of the culturally-responsive teaching framework has also sparked the emergence of a set of similarly related curricular renovations: culturally appropriate, [2] culturally congruent, [3] culturally compatible, [4] and

---

1 Gay Geneva, *Culturally Responsive Teaching: Theory, Research, and Practice* (New York, Teachers College Press, 2018).
2 Kathryn Au and Cathie Jordan, "Teaching Reading to Hawaiian Children: Finding a Culturally Appropriate Solution," *Culture and the Bilingual Classroom: Studies in Classroom Ethnography* (1981): 139-152.
3 Gerald Mohatt and Frederick Erickson, "Cultural Differences in Teaching Styles in an Odawa School: A Sociolinguistic Approach," *Culture and the Bilingual Classroom: Studies in Classroom Ethnography* (1981): 105.
4 Cathie Jordan, "Translating Culture: From Ethnographic information to Educational Program," *Anthropology & Education Quarterly* 16, no. 2 (1985): 105-123.

culturally relevant.[5]

## Gay's Influence on Current Research and Policy Solutions

The development of robust forms of democratic education, working in tandem with the development of robust forms of culturally-responsive teaching, represent two significant tools that can be recruited to address issues of alienation that many students who are culturally and/or linguistically diverse face. Teachers' misconceptions of students' cultural behaviors can lead to academic underachievement.[6]

The nation's diverse students are all too often not exposed to democratic education and instead must experience a lack of inclusive multicultural curriculum, discriminatory practices, and disproportionate representation in special education programs.[7] Too many educational programs still fail to implement decent forms of multicultural education despite accelerating levels of racial and cultural diversity within the United States.[8] As is by now well-established, Gay teaches us that educators must practice culturally responsive teaching and learn to see how the cultural characteristics and experiences of students who are ethnically diverse can function as conductors for progressive teaching.[9] The implementation of culturally-responsive teaching along with the cultivation of democratic practices and habits, Gay contends, should be used to create spaces within which students can think critically and learn in nondiscriminatory environments.[10]

Moreover, when teachers fail to connect students' culture and schooling, the risk for teacher referral for special education services increases, thus creating an unfair and disproportionate representation

5 Gloria Ladson-Billings, "Culturally Relevant Teaching: The Key to Making Multicultural Education Work," *Research and Multicultural Education: From the Margins to the Mainstream* (1992): 106-121.
6 Asa G. Hilliard, "Behavioral Style, Culture, and Teaching and Learning," *The Journal of Negro Education* 61, no. 3 (1992): 370-377.
7 Geneva Gay, *Culturally Responsive Teaching*.
8 Ibid.
9 Ibid.
10 Amy Gutmann, "Unity and Diversity in Democratic Multicultural Education," *Diversity and Citizenship Education: Global Perspectives* (2004): 71-96.

of students who are diverse in special education.[11] As researchers have by now empirically verified, teachers' perceptions and lack of cultural responsiveness often results in low academic achievement.[12] [13]

## Unique Contributions of Culturally Responsive Teaching

Culturally responsive teaching is a form of pedagogy that focuses on the inclusion of students' cultural references in all aspects of learning.[14] Culturally responsive teaching is a pedagogical approach that can help teachers cultivate practices that provide unique opportunities to implement active strategies that reflect the students' experiences, especially for those who are culturally and/or linguistically diverse.[15] Culturally responsive teaching promotes inclusion because it gives students a sense of recognition and of civic equality.[16] [17] Research indicates that the recognition and civic equality that students experience in culturally responsive classrooms help them feel included and more academically engaged.[18]

Any meaningful academic improvement among students who are culturally and ethnically diverse will be achieved only to the extent they are taught through their own cultural experiences.[19] Culturally responsive teaching in democratic classrooms are deliberative and nondiscriminatory for diverse students [20] [21] Democratic classrooms reinforce the democratic values of diversity and equality, thus opening

11 Asa G. Hilliard, "Behavioral Style, Culture, and Teaching and Learning."
12 Ibid.
13 Festus E. Obiakor, "Teacher Expectations of Minority Exceptional Learners: Impact on "Accuracy" of Self Concepts," *Exceptional Children* 66, no. 1 (1999): 39-53.
14 Geneva Gay, *Culturally Responsive Teaching*.

15 Lewis B. Jackson, Diane L. Ryndak, and Michael L. Wehmeyer, "The Dynamic Relationship between Context, Curriculum, and Student Learning: A Case for Inclusive Education as a Research-Based Practice." *Research and Practice for Persons with Severe Disabilities* 34, no. 1 (2008): 175-195.
16 Amy Gutmann, "Unity and Diversity in Democratic Multicultural Education."
17 Geneva Gay, *Culturally Responsive Teaching*.
18 Amy Gutmann, "Unity and Diversity in Democratic Multicultural Education."
19 Gloria Ladson-Billings, "What We Can Learn from Multicultural Education Research," *Educational Leadership* 51, no. 8 (1994): 22-26.
20 Amy Gutmann, "Unity and Diversity in Democratic Multicultural Education."
21 Geneva Gay, *Culturally Responsive Teaching*.

the classroom's stage for culturally responsive teaching.[22]

This volume highlights existing educational practices of culturally responsive teaching in schools throughout the United States. The authors featured in this volume discuss how they have sought to integrate culturally responsive teaching into their classroom practice for the normative aim of intellectual, social, emotional, and political empowerment.[23]

Yuan and Jiang challenge teachers to incorporate culturally responsive teaching into their curriculum, especially in increasingly multicultural classrooms, for children's cultural empowerment and academic success.[24] This book outlines how culturally responsive teaching within the educational space fosters the progression of scholars across several disciplines including disability studies, engineering, educational policy, and multicultural education. In the chapters ahead, we furnish various accounts of teachers and researchers on how culturally responsive teaching has affected the knowledge, skills, and behaviors in the field of educational leadership and policy, especially within the realm of social justice. Many authors also outline how to effectively integrate culturally responsive teaching within different ethnic enclaves. The following words from Gholdy Muhammad, who was interviewed about Gay's impact on educational theory, practice and advocacy, summarizes the point and the spirit of this book:

> We need these kinds of moments where we take on, when we say, you know, [Gay] requires our specificity at this time, you know, in her work. And I think just by honoring and saying that it's really important for her, for other Black women too. And to really build this thing up and to be supported. You know, because I cannot imagine she's had it easy at institutions, doing this work, during the time she did it, in institutions that are mostly white.

22 Amy Gutmann, "Unity and Diversity in Democratic Multicultural Education."
23 Gloria Ladson-Billings, "Culturally Relevant Teaching: The Key to Making Multicultural Education Work."
24 Ting Yuan, and Hui Jiang. "Culturally Responsive Teaching for Children from Low-Income, Immigrant Families," *Young Exceptional Children* 22, no. 3 (2019): 150-161.

*I can't imagine it's easy (chuckle). So you know, what does it take to keep that idea of joy and sustainability while you're doing that? That's really important to ask and to figure out. It's something that I'm also asking and trying to figure out too.*[25]

25 Gholdy E. Muhammad (Associate Professor of Literacy, Language, and Culture) in discussion with author, September, 2022.

# Part I

## Culturally Responsive Teaching Framework Developed by Dr. Geneva Gay

# CHAPTER 1

# Historical Context of the Culturally Responsive Teaching Framework

*By Karsonya Wise Whitehead*

*Culturally Responsive Teaching, although it is a relatively new term, has its foundation in the ongoing struggle in this country to be educated and to be free. In order to understand how it has been shaped, one must use the long eye of history to look back and then look forward.*

## The Long Eye of History

In 1654, as the nation was still in the very early stages of growth and development, the first documented Black protest happened in America. Eleven enslaved men and women living in the Council of New Netherland (later renamed New York) petitioned and won their freedom and land. They had completed seventeen of their eighteen years of indentured servitude and argued that they should be freed and not subject to the 1625 Virginia law that was beginning to be adopted in the colonies. This law distinguished between Black servitude and Black slavery and laid the groundwork for the harsher more substantial slave laws that took effect beginning in 1657. Although that was the first documented racial protest, it was not the first one to happen nor was it the last. The earliest account of a rebellion by enslaved people occurred in 1687 on a plantation in Virginia. Although the plan was discovered before it happened, the idea that Black people were beginning to plan to aggressively challenge the system is important to note. There were always two movements happening within the Black community, one which worked within and the other which worked outside of the legal system. The understanding of these two movements, really helps to frame the Black American experience. The struggle and desire to be free, to write our history, and to pursue our own destiny has long been a part of that experience and despite laws, designed to restrict rights and freedoms, it has remained a central part of the story.

During the American Civil War, enslaved and freeborn men joined the Union Army in the battle in the South while freeborn men and women were engaged in civil disobedience in the North. Within the Black community, the question was never whether they should get involved in the struggle for civil rights; but, rather when, where, and to what extent.

As America has continued to advance—from its early days as a young nation to its current role as a world power—Black people have both contributed to but have not always been able to benefit from the collective advancement. These struggles and protests did not just involve fighting for land and physical freedom, it also extended to the classroom. The questions around educating Black people and centering our experience have been asked since the beginning of this American experiment and in so many ways, are still being asked today. Who has the right to receive an education? Should Black people benefit from the American educational system? What history should be taught? And is Black history American history? On the surface, using a 21st century lens, the answers are simple: Everyone. Yes. The entire story. And yes, Black history is American history. But if one were to use the long eye of history, then the questions of education become more entangled with questions of freedom, of self-determination, of the American story. Frederick Douglass said that "Once you learn to read, you will be forever free." So, the conversation about education is not about education but about people. This tension that existed between working for something and not receiving it has naturally led to reoccurring movements for civil rights.

It was happening in the courtroom in 1849, with the Roberts v. City of Boston case, as lawyers unsuccessfully argued that legalized segregation psychologically damaged black students; and on the streetcars in 1867 when Caroline Le Count, a freeborn educated woman, engaged in civil disobedience to force the city to enforce the law that integrated public transportation. It happened in 1851 when Sojourner Truth, at the Women's Rights Convention in Akron, Ohio challenged everyone to think about the rights of women and again one year later when Frederick Douglass challenged Americans to think about the significance of the fourth of July in the lives and experiences of enslaved people. The early movement for civil rights from the cotton fields in the South to the cotton shirts in the North was extremely active and provided the roots upon which the modern Civil Rights Movement was built.

While they worked within the system, Black people have also openly rebelled against the establishment. In order to narrow the scope of the discussion, the modern Civil Rights Movement, in this essay, begins with the 1954 Brown v. Board of Education decision. It peaks in 1957 with President Eisenhower's signing of the Civil Rights Act of 1957 and continues into the 1960s starting with the Boynton v. Virginia case that ruled that segregation in bus terminals was unconstitutional and begins to decline around 1972 with the first National Black Political Convention. The battleground then was over laws, practices, policies and procedures. It was a battle to get America to live up to its creed and to its promises of meaningful freedom for Black people. Dr. King in his "I Have a Dream" speech said, "America has given the Negro people a bad check, a check which has come back marked 'insufficient funds.'" The fight was about trying to get our check cashed.

That was then and one could argue that though the check has not been cashed (because reparations have not been paid), there have been substantial political gains from the election of President Barack Obama, the confirmation of Supreme Court Justice Ketanji Brown Jackson, the election of House Speaker Hakeem Jeffries, and the recent election of Governor Wes Moore; and some educational gains as Black women are currently among the most educated group in America. The battlegrounds have shifted and within this new model, I believe that are three battlegrounds where we must take our last stand. These are the spaces in which we must hold fast. The first is the evangelical Christian church where there are ongoing debates and discussions about the role of the church in determining the moral direction of this country. After the recent ruling in the Dobbs v. Jackson Women's Health Organization Supreme Court case—which overturned Roe v. Wade thereby giving individual states the authority to regulate abortion—politicians have continued to conflate morality, politics, and race. Despite the historical understanding of the separation of church and state, which is loosely grounded in the First Amendment and has been held up by rulings by SCOTUS, the evangelical church (through both the election of far-right Christian politicians and the appointment of Supreme Court judges) has continued to expand its political influence.

The second is the voting booth. In 1965, one year after the signing of the Civil Rights Act, President Lyndon B. Johnson signed the Voting Rights Act, which outlawed the discriminatory voting practices (i.e., literacy tests, poll taxes, the grandfather clause, etc.) which were adopted in many southern states after the Civil War, into law. It was described by many as one of the most far-reaching pieces of civil rights legislation in American history. The Act was designed to enforce the voting rights that were guaranteed by the Fourteenth and Fifteen Amendments and has been amended by Congress five times to expand its protection. At the same time, there has been and continues to be a concentrated effort by SCOTUS to limit the scope of the

Act. It was in 2013, with the Shelby County v. Holder decision that Section 4(b) of the Act was ruled unconstitutional giving nine states, located mostly in the South, the authority to change their election laws without advance federal approval. It is important to note that seven of the nine states—Alabama, Georgia, Louisiana, Mississippi, South Carolina, Texas and Virginia—were a part of the Confederacy.

The final battleground is the classroom. Frederick Douglass in his autobiography writes that he once overheard plantation owner, Hugh Auld, explaining to his wife Sophia why she should not teach a young Douglass how to read, "Learning will spoil the best n*gger in the world. If he learns to read the Bible, it will forever unfit him to be a slave.... If you teach him how to read, he'll want to know how to write, and this accomplished, he'll be running away with himself." This fear of people who were enslaved choosing to free themselves was uniquely tied to them being educated. In the minds of some plantation owners, education was the cornerstone to claiming one's freedom. For them learning how to read led to learning how to write which led to the ability (and the courage) to forge free papers and then use them to free themselves. These were harsh laws, punishable by death but it did not stop Black people from finding ways to circumvent the system so that they could receive their education. Whether it was trading bread for education (Douglass' method) or setting up makeshift schools in the woods or in the cabins of people who were enslaved, education was at least one of the "North Stars" for people who were enslaved.

Post Reconstruction, national concerns seemed to be directed towards reunifying the Nation and not on either educating or training the close to four million people who had been enslaved. Education even after freedom was still very difficult to attain. The Supreme Court, which had many justices from the South, began the task of eroding the rights that had been granted to Black people through the Reconstruction Amendments. The 1896 Plessy v. Ferguson "separate but equal" decision, that legally sanctioned southern practices of racial discrimination in public accommodations, has its roots in the

Supreme Court's 1883 outlawing of the 1875 Civil Rights Act and the 1873 Slaughter-House cases, where the Supreme Court ruled that the Fourteenth Amendment protected federal civil rights and not the civil rights that "heretofore belonged to the states." With the Plessy ruling, the Supreme Court upheld segregation and the South's "Jim Crow Laws" continued without question. In addition, the lynching of Black men and in some few instances black women and white sympathizers, continued to occur at an average of 150.4 per year.

This system of laws and social customs that reinforced racial segregation and discrimination, continued to spread unchecked and continued to restrict the economic, educational and social progress of Black Americans. Yet, within this environment of institutionalized racism, Black Americans continued to build church communities, establish educational institutions, organize legal campaigns and establish and operate national and international businesses. Many of the leadership and organizational skills nurtured among Black Americans would serve them later during the Civil Rights Movement, in leadership and organizational successes, despite the policies and practices of a southern (and to a great extent, northern) white society violently resistant to the extension of equality to its Black American citizens.

In 1954, after a series of local and state cases had been argued by the NAACP Legal Defense and Educational Fund, Inc., the Supreme Court in the Brown decision ruled that segregated public schools violated the Fourteenth Amendment. As a direct response to the ruling, several white-only groups were organized with the intention of "maintaining a decent southern way of life...that placed Black people in subordinate roles." One year later, the Supreme Court, in what is commonly called the Brown II decision, rejected the NAACP's plan to integrate instantly and totally and instead adopted the Justice Department's "go slow" approach. This plan to allow integration to happen "with all deliberate speed" translated into the enactment of 145 laws to prevent desegregation. The response to these laws, which included the Montgomery Bus Boycott among many others, were early organized efforts that provided the foundation that the Civil Rights Movement needed to build upon. The work to openly challenge and dismantle segregation had begun and would not stop until it was done. What was becoming blatantly obvious to the Black community was that there was a difference between de jure and de facto segregation. In Little Rock, Arkansas, for example, it took one thousand federal troops and ten thousand National Guard members for nine Black students to integrate Central High School in the fall of 1957. This was the true face of integration…nine Black students attempting to go to school in a population of thousands.

In 1960, the Civil Rights Movement was galvanized by the decision of four young college students to sit down and request service at Woolworth's segregated lunch counter in downtown Greensboro, NC. This first sit-in sparked the beginning of a grassroots movement, which was primarily led by Black students, against segregated public spaces in the South. In less than two weeks, the nonviolent sit-in strategy had spread across the South. Within a year, an estimated 70,000 Black or racially integrated student groups had participated in or marched in support of sit-ins throughout the country. This wave of nonviolent protesting was met by escalating, often violent, resistance from angry white mobs, at times openly supported by the local police, whose tactics included using water hoses, throwing acid, massive armed arrests and beatings. It had become clear to many of the young people working with the established civil rights groups, such as the Congress of Racial Equality (CORE), SCLC and the NAACP, that they needed their own student-led organization, and with the assistance of SCLC activist Ella Baker, they created the Student Nonviolent Coordinating Committee (SNCC). As the grassroots movement fought racism head-on, Black people continued to confront segregation through the court system or through the Executive and Legislative branches of government or within the classroom. These were the struggles that led to policy changes but even though there have been gains, the battle for the classroom remains.

## Where To Go From Here

Carter G. Woodson in his 1933 book "The Mis-Education of the Negro" wrote, "The education of the Negroes, then, the most important thing in the uplift of the Negroes, is almost entirely in the hands of those who have enslaved them and now segregate them." This cuts to the heart of the problem. If the education of Black people is filtered through what Toni Morrison described as the "white gaze," then education will never be used to free minds, challenge hearts, and motivate young people to set the world on fire. It is obvious that something else was needed, a different way of viewing our history, ourselves, and our classrooms. In 2021, the National Assessment of Educational Progress (NAEP), a sector of the U.S. Department of Education, noted that 84 percent of Black students lack proficiency in mathematics and 85 percent of Black students lack proficiency in reading skills—which is astonishing particularly because in 1870, five years after the ending of slavery, 79.9 percent of Black people could not read nor write.

This is why Gloria Ladson-Billings' work in Culturally Relevant Teaching, a pedagogy that is grounded and rooted in teachers' practice of cultural competence, is so ground-breaking. It is not just that it is necessary, it is the net that is needed to both catch Black students to train them and then set them free. Where Ladson-Billings' work stopped, is where Geneva Gay's started. In her book, Culturally Responsive Teaching: Theory, Research, and Practice, Gay expanded the traditional understanding and description of culture beyond just the pillars of race and ethnicity. Gay noted that, "Even without being consciously aware of it, culture determines how we think, believe, and behave." It determines how we move in the world, how we see ourselves, and how we see others.

In order to understand the full scope of the importance and significance of Dr. Gay's impact on the field, one must use a comparative media analysis. María Colompos-Tohtsonie in her extensive unpublished research of Gay's legacy in "The Transformation of her 'Culturally Responsive Teaching' Theory on Research, Policy, and

Practice" provides us with a blueprint that captures the full extent of Gay's work, starting with a timeline that shows how her work directly addressed many of the concerns about the miseducation of Black children:

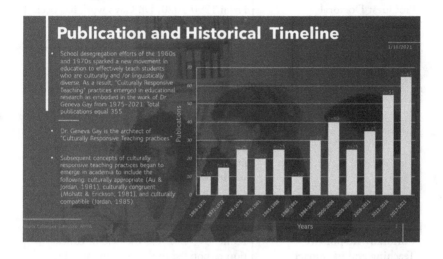

## The Impact of Dr. Gay's Work

| | |
|---|---|
| **Overview of Dr. Gay's Textual Lineage** | From 1968-2021, Dr. Gay published more than 300 articles, book chapters, monographs, and book reviews in the area of multicultural education. |
| **ProQuest Doctoral Dissertation Citation Rate** | From 1990-2020, Dr. Gay's work has been cited in approximately 106,448 doctoral dissertations. |
| **WorldCat Book Publication Data[1]** | Between 2000-2018, there were three editions of Gay's book *Culturally responsive teaching: Theory, research, and practice* published. The book is currently housed in 3,115 WorldCat member libraries worldwide.<br>*Becoming multicultural educators: Personal journey toward professional agency*, is housed in 569 WorldCat member libraries<br>*Expressively Black: The cultural basis of ethnic identity* is housed in 457 WorldCat member libraries worldwide. |
| **Culturally Responsive Teaching and its impact on schools** | From 1975-2021, as the field of education responded to the need to include "Culturally Responsive Teaching" Culturally Responsive Teaching practices, there were 355 Culturally Responsive Teaching publications. |

---

1 http://worldcat.org/identities/lccn-n82049747/

Using Colompos-Tohtsonie's research as a starting point, provides us with the metric that we need to understand the full impact of Dr. Gay's work and how it has transformed the field and transformed teachers and students. Culturally Responsive Teaching is thus much more than just a tool to be used in the classroom, it is a guideline for how we can see ourselves in this society and how we can imagine a way forward. It is both a lens and a prism and despite the ways in which Black history has been marginalized, Culturally Responsive Teaching teaches us that in order to move forward, it must be moved to the center. It is more than just a bridge to get us over, it is the foundation that we need to build upon. [26]

## Endnotes

1 For complete timeline see Charles M. Christian, Black Saga: The African American Experience (New York: Houghton Mifflin Company, 1995), 9 -15.

2 John Hope Franklin's book, From Slavery to Freedom, mentions the 1687 rebellion discussion, however, Black Saga does not document it. It is noted that the 1522 slave revolt in Hispaniol and the 1526 slave revolt in the San Miguel settlement (South Carolina), both predate the Virginia discussion. See Black Saga and John Hope Franklin, Jr. and Alfred Moss, Jr. From Slavery to Freedom: A History of African Americans 8th edition (New York: Alfred P. Knopf, 2004) for further information.

3 Frederick Douglass, The Life and Times of Frederick Douglass, (Mineola: Dover Publications, 2003).

4 Benjamin Roberts' case was argued by Robert Morris, a young Black lawyer, and Charles Sumner, who later authored the Civil Rights Act of 1875. Although they did not win, five years later, it did have a direct impact on the Massachusetts 1855 ruling against segregated public schools. "Segregation in the United States," Microsoft® Encarta® Online Encyclopedia 2006 http://encarta.msn.com © 1997-2006 Microsoft Corporation

5 It is difficult to set and agree upon an exact year that the Movement began to decline. On the surface, it appears as if it is as easy to choose 1972 as it is to choose 1973, when the Supreme Court ruled in the Keyes v. Denver School District case that integration must also take place in non-southern school systems. Below the surface, 1972 was selected for a number of specific reasons: this was the first year that Black income had risen substantially since 1960 (obviously as a direct result of the gains within the struggle) particularly in the South where there was 9% increase in household incomes; Benjamin L. Hooks became the first Black person to serve on the Federal Communications Commission (FCC); President Richard Nixon rejected the idea of busing to achieve school segregation; the Supreme Court ruled in the Wright v. City of Emporia and Cotton v. Schotland Neck Board of Education cases that schools could not switch school districts to avoid segregating and Barbara Jordan became the first Black women representative to be elected to the U.S. Congress. Additionally (and in a lot of ways, most importantly), although Black people continued to struggle for equality, the way that they

26 https://nces.ed.gov/nationsreportcard/subject/publications/stt2019/pdf/2020013VA8.pdf, https://nces.ed.gov/naal/lit_history.asp

26 Geneva Gay, Culturally Responsive Teaching: Theory, Research, and Practice. (New York: Teachers College Press, 2018).

struggled had changed. The mass mobilizations, the Marches and the number of civil arrests did decline and have not increased since then. Christian, Black Saga, 458-462

6 Douglass, The Life and Times of Frederick Douglass.

7 Christian, Black Saga, 243

8 Jim Crow, as it well known and documented, was not a real person but a minstrel song that had been written during the 19th Century (although there has been some discussion that the actor modeled Jim Crow after a slave that he had met). It was picked up by a newspaper and quickly became the "name" for America's apartheid system. See http://www.pbs.org/wnet/jimcrow/ for further information.

9 These figures document the years between 1882 and 1900. Christian notes that the number began to decrease after 1900 with the a) increase in public awareness; b) the fear of legal consequences and c) the crusade against lynching by writers such as Ida Wells Barnett, a Black female editor and co-owner of the Memphis Free Speech newspaper. Christian, Black Saga, 262

10 The First Church of Colored Baptists was established in 1725 when Virginia granted Black slaves the right to have their own church in Williamsburg, VA. Ibid, 33

11 Ashmun Institute (later renamed Lincoln University) opened on January 1, 1854, as the first Black college charted it the United States. Ibid, 157

12 Despite the shared names, the NAACP and the NAACP Legal Defense and Educational Fund are two separate organizations. The Fund is a legal aid group that argues on behalf of the NAACP and other civil rights groups. For further information, read histories of Brown v. Board, Thurgood Marshall and Constance Baker Motley.

13 The Oliver Brown et al vs. the Board of Education, Topeka, Kansas case consisted of five cases from around the country: Belton (Bulah) v. Gebhart from Delaware, Bolling v. Sharpe from Washington, DC, Briggs v. Elliot from South Carolina and Davis v. County School Board of Prince Edward County from Virginia.

14 Peter B. Levy, The Civil Rights Movement (Connecticut: Greenwood Press, 1998), 387.

15 De jure segregation generally refers to segregation that is directly intended or mandated by law or segregation which has had the sanction of law. De facto segregation is segregation which is inadvertent and without assistance of school authorities and not caused by state action, but rather by social, economic and other determinates. Henry Campbell Black, Black's Law Dictionary 6th edition (Minnesota: West Publishing Company, 1990), 416 & 425 or see "Segregation in the United States" at http://encarta.msn.com for further information.

16 In 1958, The Little Rock Nine, as they came to be known, were awarded the NAACP's Spingarn Medal for bravery. One year later, Ernest Green, the oldest one in the group, became the first Black person to graduate from Central High.

17 Ezell Blair, Jr., David Richmond, Franklin McCain and Joseph McNeil were students at North Carolina A&T University. Although the managers refused to serve them and they faced mounting white resistance, they returned and sat down for five days straight.

18 The actual numbers show that the sit-in movement spread to 15 different cities in five southern states.

19 Christian, Black Saga, 405.

20 See We Shall Not Be Moved lesson plan at https://www.visionaryproject.org/teacher/lesson2/overview.html for further information about Baker.

21 https://nces.ed.gov/nationsreportcard/subject/publications/stt2019/pdf/2020013VA8.pdf, https://nces.ed.gov/naal/lit_history.asp

22 Geneva Gay, Culturally Responsive Teaching: Theory, Research, and Practice. (New York: Teachers College Press, 2018).

# CHAPTER 2

# How Researchers Within the Field of Culturally Responsive Pedagogy Have Expanded Upon the Culturally Responsive Teaching Framework

*By Joseph E. Flynn & Sarah Militz-Frielink*

It is near impossible to have a discussion about multicultural education, or education generally, without mentioning the work and ideas of Geneva Gay. As the creator of the idea of *culturally responsive teaching*,[27] [28] [29] Gay has published approximately 360 articles, books, book chapters, monographs, and book reviews in the area of multicultural education, making her one of the most cited experts in the field. Her research has had a profound influence on how we think of education and the relationship between pedagogy and instruction and the importance of recognizing and responding to culture in the classroom. Her work has been crucial not only to our national dialogues about multicultural education but also equity-based pedagogies and practices. In fact, Gay's work has transcended the boundaries

27 Gay Geneva, *Culturally Responsive Teaching: Theory, Research, and Practice* (New York, Teachers College Press, 2018)
28 Geneva Gay, "The What, Why, and How of Culturally Responsive Teaching: International Mandates, Challenges, and Opportunities," *Multicultural Education Review* 7, no. 3 (2015): 123-139.
29 Geneva Gay, "Preparing for Culturally Responsive Teaching," *Journal of Teacher Education* 53, no. 2 (2002): 106-116.

of the United States to being embraced by the international education community. This is sensible. Gay's work has inspired generations of students, teacher educators, curriculum scholars, activists, administrators, and other education professionals, providing the language and theoretical and practical foundations to answer one of the most basic and intractable questions in education: How do we best teach in a manner that embraces, respects, and responds to the unique, diverse cultures in our schools and be more intentionally responsive to persistent equity gaps between White students and their non-White counterparts?

The central focus of Geneva Gay's research is transforming how educators work with African, Asian, Latino, and Native American students in U.S. schools. Gay believes that systemic reforms must be made to increase students' academic, social, psychological, and emotional achievement within different subject areas across various school levels.[30] Gay discusses how to reverse the underachievement of students of color.[31] She proposes that all teachers implement culturally responsive teaching in their classroom to improve the education of students of color who are marginalized:

> Culturally responsive teaching is defined as using the cultural characteristics, experiences, and perspectives of ethnically diverse students as conduits for teaching them more effectively. It is based on the assumption that when academic knowledge and skills are situated within the lived experiences and frames of reference of students, they are more personally meaningful, have higher interest appeal, and are learned more easily and thoroughly.[32]

In short, culture matters. That may seem like an obvious sentiment, but a part of the reason it seems obvious is a direct result of the power and substance of Gay's ideas and presence. She has been a significant north star – so to speak – to the advocates for equitable

30 Gay Geneva, *Culturally Responsive Teaching: Theory, Research, and Practice.*
31 Ibid, 1.
32 Gay Geneva, "Preparing for Culturally Responsive Teaching," 106.

educational thought and practice, as evidenced by the contents of this volume's preface, introduction, and first chapter.

This chapter celebrates the impact that Geneva Gay's legacy has had on well-known professors in multicultural and social justice education and by extension the field of education at large. Through interviews with noted education theorists, researchers, and practitioners, Gay's contribution of culturally responsive teaching, her impact on educational theory, practice, and advocacy, and the importance of her presence as an African American woman in the field are brought fully to light. This chapter also explores Gay's work as an anti-racist framework for educators in today's hostile political climate. The interviews were based on the following questions:

- When did you first encounter Geneva Gay's work and what were your early reactions to learning about her?

- How have your interactions with Gay influenced your career and professional choices?

- In what ways has Gay's work on culturally responsive teaching influenced your scholarly identity?

- In today's political climate we see a number of states moving to illegalize or ban critical race theory and other states are passing laws using similar language banning lessons that create any discomfort, guilt, or anguish based on an aspect of a student's identity. How does Gay's work counter this legislative era?

- Geneva Gay is one of the most cited educational theorists. How would you describe Gay's influence on educational thought and practice? How do you envision the role of culturally responsive teaching as we continue into the 21st century?

- Gay is one of the most significant figures in educational

thought and practice and she carries on the strong tradition of excellence in African American's contribution to the field. Can you speak to the importance of Geneva Gay being a Black woman in education thought and practice?

- Finally, do you have any concluding thoughts about Geneva Gay and her work that we have not covered thus far?

The following scholars contributed their thoughts, insights and reflections on Dr. Gay's legacy: Christine Sleeter, David Kirkland, Dorinda J. Carter-Andrews, David Stovall, and Gholdy Muhammad. The forthcoming discussion will unfold as reflections about Dr. Gay and her legacy.

## Christine Sleeter

Another towering figure in multicultural education, Christine Sleeter has been on the forefront of advancing multicultural education theory and practice since the 1980s. As a teacher, teacher educator, author, speaker, activist, and blogger, Dr. Sleeter has published over 150 articles, books, and journals that help others explore "teachers as they grapple with improving their ability to reach and teach their diverse students."[33] She has developed several frameworks and tools to guide educators, such as her tools for Critical Family History, and the framework in her best-selling book (with J. Flores Carmona) *Un-Standardizing Curriculum*."[34] Generally, Sleeter's research and scholarship delves into anti-racist multicultural education, ethnic studies, and teacher education.

Now a Professor Emerita in the College of Education at California State University-Monterey Bay, Sleeter continues to be a key figure with a profound impact in multicultural education.[35] Her impact on multicultural education is on par with many of the other greats: James

---

33 "Christine Sleeter," Biography, accessed September 21, 2022, https://www.christinesleeter.org/biography.
34 Ibid.
35 Ibid.

Banks, Gloria Ladson-Billings, Carl Grant, Sonia Nieto, and others. As she stated, "Sometimes people think of me and Dr. Gay as being contemporaries, and in a way, I guess we are. Both of us have been around in the field of multicultural education for a long time, but she precedes me, and in many ways I feel like her shoulders are some of the shoulders that I stand on."[36]

Sleeter, with a spark of nostalgia and pure joy in her eye, described Geneva Gay as a great role model who influenced her from the very first interaction:

> *I first became aware of her when I was a classroom teacher in Seattle (during the latter 1970s) and I was taking a course in multicultural education, maybe one of the first to be offered. And it was part of my master's program through Seattle University. Somebody had gotten Dr. Gay to come in and talk with teachers, and I was just blown away by her. I was so, I mean, you've heard her speak, how she takes ideas and elaborates on them in very insightful ways.*[37]

However, it was not until she began her doctoral study with Dr. Carl Grant at the University of Wisconsin that she had the opportunity to get to know Dr. Gay, "It was not long after that that I went to Graduate School at the University of Wisconsin-Madison, working with Carl Grant, who knew her, and then I was able to start getting to know her personally through the work that Carl was doing."[38]

The role of Geneva Gay's work on culturally responsive teaching was a profound influence on her. She went on to say:

> *... whenever I'm writing or giving a definition of culturally responsive pedagogy, which in a lot of my work I do, [Dr. Gay is] the first person whose work I go to ... One of the things in that book (Geneva Gay's watershed*

---

36 Christine Sleeter (Professor Emerita in the College of Education at California State University Monterey Bay) in discussion with the author, September, 2022.
37 Ibid.
38 Ibid.

*text, Culturally Responsive Teaching),[39] I remember that struck me and stayed with me when I picked it up is, I think it's her second chapter that's on caring (for clarity's sake it is the third chapter of the 3rd edition), and I don't always necessarily see people lead with relationships and care as the basis of pedagogy, and the fact that she did that in that book and sort of made that a foundational concept that the rest of pedagogy is built on resonates with me and I draw on that sometimes."[40]*

Sleeter also spoke about the conversations she has had with Gay over the years, and how one of the points Geneva made that really resonated with her was about people's misconceptions of multicultural education. "People tend to think of multicultural education as this thing that's over here, rather than as a way of understanding everything in the education enterprise."[41] That is no small differentiation. The idea that multicultural education *is* education is crucial, especially in today's political climate and the recurring pushback on pedagogies and practices that support the educational advancement of historically marginalized groups.

When asked about anti-critical race theory and/or anti-diversity legislation and Geneva Gay research as a counter to such legislation, Sleeter spoke of Geneva's work as a tool that speaks back to the legislation.

> *Today, legislators are talking about not making kids feel uncomfortable because of who they are, and yet they're banning the very things that help kids of color feel comfortable in a classroom ... Her work, and especially her book, on culturally responsive pedagogy? She grounds it in research. Since it is grounded in research, it at least gives people the tools to be able to speak back to the*

39 Geneva Gay, *Culturally Responsive Teaching: Theory, Research, and Practice.*
40 Christine Sleeter (Professor Emerita in the College of Education at California State University Monterey Bay) in discussion with the author, September, 2022.
41 Ibid.

*legislation, and this whole chilling effect that is happening because of the sort of anti-critical race theory stuff.*[42]

Sleeter went on to discuss how she envisioned culturally responsive teaching in the 21st century. She said that "you just can't talk about pedagogy in the abstract."[43] She emphasized that if you are talking about pedagogy, it must be *responsive* to somebody. "It's in relationship to somebody, with the question being who is it in relationship to and in Gay's thinking about culturally responsive pedagogy in many ways, what she's doing, I think, is re-theorizing pedagogy."[44] Sleeter deliberated about the right-wing political attacks that will keep coming in the 21st century, but stressed the power of diversity in the classroom that will remain:

> *It does take us into the 21st century, especially with the diversification of the student population and the current attacks that we're experiencing right now. Those kinds of attacks have been happening for a long time, and they'll come, they'll be powerful, and then something else will take over. And so with this, something else will take over, but what won't change is the continued diversification of the students.*[45]

When Sleeter was asked about the importance of Geneva Gay being a Black woman in the field, she pointed to the fact that Gay's work is informed by her experiences as a Black woman. "I think that's why she is so insistent that multicultural education have race be the center, and that I mean the work grows out of who she is, but the other thing is that she in many ways challenges stereotypes that people may have of who Black women are and what Black women can do."[46]

## David Kirkland

---

42 Ibid.
43 Ibid.
44 Ibid.
45 Ibid.
46 Ibid.

David Kirkland is an activist, educator, cultural critic, and author. Currently, he is an Associate Professor of English and Urban Education at New York University. Taking a transdisciplinary approach, his scholarship covers many topics including: school climate and discipline; school integration and choice; culture and education; vulnerable learners; and intersections among race, gender, and education.[47] Throughout his interview, Kirkland had many powerful statements about Geneva Gay's theory on culturally responsive teaching, Geneva Gay's influence on educational thought and practice, the impact of Gay's work on his scholarship, and her work as an anti-racist framework for educators in today's hostile political climate. In terms of his first reactions to Geneva Gay's theory on culturally responsive teaching, Kirkland discussed how the term just resonated with him and how "this concept of education should be responsive to the cultural needs of the individuals by which teachers serve." He spoke of how "we should utilize those things through which young people live and create and become in concert with–this practice that we call cognitive transformation."[48]

Kirkland opened by unabashedly admitting that he first heard about her without knowing it was her. "The term just resonated. Education should be responsive to students' needs. Most of us know about her but not her name." That disconnect is not necessarily uncommon. He first began to use culturally responsive teaching methods as an English teacher in Detroit, using hip hop lyrics to engage African American youth in literacy practices and acquisition. It is arguable that any educator who tries to embrace and be responsive to the cultural needs of their students is embracing the work of Geneva Gay, even if they do not know her name or the name of her idea. By the time Kirkland arrived in graduate school at Michigan State University and began to delve into Dr. Gay's work, his mind was proverbially

47 "David Kirkland," New York University Steinhardt, accessed September 14, 2022, https://steinhardt.nyu.edu/people/david-kirkland.

48 David Kirkland (Associate Professor of English and Urban Education) in discussion with the author, September, 2022.

blown and expanded, forever changing the way he conceived of education, teaching, the role of culture in the classroom, and his mission as an educator. Gay essentially validated his ideas and presence in the academy and the field. Kirkland revealed a salient question that culturally responsive teaching raised for him in the classroom: "The question there was how do we respond to the cultural needs of our young people as a way to transform their educational experience in ways that may enlighten not only their engagement, but the possibility of their performance within the classroom?"[49]

Reminiscing about Geneva Gay's speech at a conference he organized when he was Executive Director of New York University Metro Center, the Metropolitan Center for Research on Equity and Transformation of Schools, he reflected on their conversation following her presentation and spoke to the personal effect Geneva Gay has had on his scholar identity. His respect and admiration for Geneva Gay brilliantly shined through the conversation:

> *Thank you for being you. Thank you for having the courage to stand. Thank you for opening up a conversation in which we would change the direction by which education, not just for Black, Brown, indigenous or otherwise vulnerable young people would be talked about or established, but the way we actually sit here and understand how learning manifests—what learning is. Because of you, because of your insight, and because people like you, scholars like me exist.*[50]

That final sentiment, "because of people like you, scholars like me exist," is an honest testament to the scope and depth of Gay's influence.

He continued to credit Geneva Gay for his achievements. "I haven't accomplished one thing on my own. It is because of people like Dr. Gay, you know?" Kirkland described how culturally responsive

---

49 Ibid.
50 Ibid.

education shaped his scholarship on the cultural lives of young Black men, and how without Gay's research he could not have focused on the asset points that recognize value in deeply understanding the cultural practices of vulnerable people. "Without Geneva's work, this kind of asset gaze (as opposed to a deficit gaze) would never have been established or allowed within educational scholarship."[51] Kirkland's declaration of appreciation was reminiscent of the same level of appreciation discussed by the chapter authors in this volume. For us, it is clear how foundational Gay is not only to the field, but also to our personal understandings and orientations to supporting the brilliance of all students, if one is so inclined to look past old and oppressive norms, stereotypes, and deficit orientations. Kirkland illuminated how Geneva Gay's theory on culturally responsive teaching shifted educational thought and practice from a deficit-based perspective on African American students to a strength-based perspective.

> So in the literacy conversation, it was about how young Black men couldn't read, or how they couldn't write? It was always deficit, how they were criminalized, how they were misbehaving. What Geneva's work gives us is a shift in perspective.[52]

Kirkland, who wrote a policy on culturally sustaining education for the state of New York, explained how people across the globe embrace culturally responsive teaching and have integrated this concept into their research, pedagogy, and practice. Having engaged with scholars all over the world who espouse Geneva Gay's theory and practice he has been exposed to the reach of Gay's revolutionary ideas.

> Not only might she be the most cited individual in the Academy, her work has taken hold across the country, if not the globe. I can go to, and I was recently in, South Africa and they're talking about culturally responsive education. I was in London and they were talking about

---

51 Ibid.
52 Ibid.

*culturally responsive education. You know, I had conver-*
*sations with, you know, Indian colleagues and they were*
*talking about culturally responsive education in New*
*York State. Django Paris' entire work around cultur-*
*ally sustaining education is based on Geneva Gay's work*
*around culturally responsive education, which is being*
*imported inside our schools. So from a pragmatic, intel-*
*lectual standpoint, the people who are engaged in edu-*
*cational practice, not just academic theorization, have*
*taken up this concept because it makes sense to them.*[53]

When asked about Geneva Gay's work as a counter to current legislation that bans the teaching of critical race theory in schools, Kirkland immediately situated Gay's work outside the white gaze. He said that he did not want to frame Gay's work as a response to whiteness, but rather that her work comes from a different place. "I think that [her work] emanates from a place of deep love and respect, resisting invisibility for people who have been obscured through the lenses in the vein of white supremacy." Kirkland continued to discuss different scholars who have affirmed this deep love and respect for the Black body. "So if we begin to think about Marc Lamont Hill's work about the expandability of Black people and Michelle Alexander's work, Django Paris, his work, and Bettina Love who really talks about how Black bodies matter–against the force of our deletion, right?" He then reiterated the role of Geneva Gay's work in the conversation about Black bodies. "If we think about white supremacy and the gaze of white supremacy as manufacturing the erasure of not only Black lives, the themes, the substance of our life, right? I think that Geneva Gay's work has emanated from a different place. It emanated from a place of Black love and Black substance, that we matter."[54]

He went on to illustrate two reasons why her representation in the field as an African American woman is so pivotal. He first pointed

53 Ibid.
54 Ibid.

out that he was raised by his grandmother who was the mother of the community. He spoke to how Black women have stood in the gaps, "not just for Black people, but for entire communities."[55] He also spoke from his perspective as a Black man recognizing the brilliance and experience of Black women who have impacted educational theory and practice. Here we must quote at length:

> *They nurse the babies, you know, of white people. Not only during chattel slavery, but even after, they've raised communities. They've held up faith traditions within African American communities. They have defined, established, you know, and pursued the hope that we get to cling to today, right? You know, so I think that it's appropriate, you know, that Geneva gay is a black woman. But, I also think that there's something about the brilliance within black women, the experience of black women that usually goes unheard not only in mainstream society, often by black men, that we have to, you know, pause, recognize, apologize for not recognizing more fully earlier ... Who has survived? Who sits right now in the shadow of amazing Black women? Who stands on the shoulders of amazing Black women? I understand firsthand the work of Black women that have given birth not only to transformation and change, but the kinds of ideas that are leading in education today.*[56]

Kirkland discussed a second reason why Geneva Gay's representation as a Black woman is so vital to the academy. He opined about Geneva Gay's contributions to Black feminism and the meaning of her work:

> *From the pragmatic standpoint I can understand as a Black man. From an intellectual standpoint, also understand that the counter-narrative that Black feminism*

55 Ibid.
56 Ibid.

34

*gives not only to patriarchy and the male gaze and the centering of this patriarchal discourse within education, but also the white gaze and everything that combines this kind of intersectional reality that lives is the experience of Black women. It's kind of an organic Black feminism. The ways that it conjures up new ideas that get us closer to a reality that centers things like care and self-love and moves us away from some of the vocabulary some of the visualization of the world that is response to a white supremacist gaze. It becomes extremely important to uphold, so what it says. The other contribution of Geneva Gay, why it's important that she's a Black woman, is that she comes to the conversation from a different positionality. She comes to the conversation from a different vantage point, and that different vantage point leads us to a truth, gives us a reality. It gives us a sense of the world that is otherwise and has otherwise never been hacked, even when black men were venerated in the academy, there was always something missing. That's the counter narrative, right? This kind of intersectional counter narrative, this kind of intersectional gaze was never fully had because we enjoyed male privilege.*[57]

As the interview began to wind down, Dr. Kirkland put a final period on his appreciation for Gay and her work. We will let his words close this section:

*The recognition of the work is long overdue. But to be sure, the work of Geneva Gay is not about Geneva Gay. It's not about a person. It's not even about an idea. The idea is important, but it's answering a question about how do we educate young people that we have long failed, to be sure our babies aren't broken, but too often the systems that we send them to are. How do we educate*

---

57 Ibid.

*our babies? How do we? How do we educate our children? Geneva says that they matter. That we must love them. That we must cultivate and create around them using the substance of our heart, knitting together the quilt that can go around them so they can endure as they grow up. She's saying that they matter, and because they matter collectively, we matter. There's an African proverb, and I'll leave you on this, that says, "If you want to go fast, go alone. But if you want to go far, go together." Geneva's work says two things. Our babies matter. We should love them. And the second thing is that because our babies matter, we matter. We matter. And we can educate them. Thank you.[58]*

## Dorinda J. Carter Andrews

Dorinda Carter Andrews is the chairperson for the Department of Teacher Education at Michigan State University. She is also a professor of race, culture, and equity. Her research is focused on racial justice and educational equity. She examines issues of racial justice in P-12 learning contexts and on college campuses, urban teacher preparation and identity development, and critical race praxis with K-12 educators. Her scholarship examines these issues by illuminating voices of youth and adults who have been historically and traditionally marginalized in schools and society.[59]

Carter Andrews revealed that she first encountered Gay's work when she was a doctoral student doing her work around trying to "better understand the experiences of Black students in predominantly white schools."[60] She then elaborated on her reactions to Gay's book on culturally responsive teaching. "I was a former teacher—a high school math teacher. So as I started reading, it's a specific chapter

58 Ibid.
59 "Dorinda Carter Andrews," Michigan State University, accessed September 19, 2022, https://education.msu.edu/people/andrews-dorinda-carter/.
60 Dorinda Carter Andrews (Chairperson for the Department of Teacher Education) in discussion with the author, September, 2022.

in Gay's book where she lays out the components or tenants of cultur- ally responsive teaching. I was like, okay, this resonates with me–both with my own pedagogy and practice."

When asked about the impact Gay's scholarship had on Carter Andrews' career and professional choices, Carter Andrews said Gay's work has both informed her epistemological standpoint in terms of her thinking critically about how she comes to know what she knows, but also how she helps students come to know what they know. "How do I model that as an educator? Future teachers and teacher educa- tors that I am working with see it in me and then can say, 'Okay, this is theory to practice, right?'" Carter Andrews further expounded on the impact of Gay's theories on her educational thought and prac- tice. "Gay's work has both illuminated for me my own epistemolog- ical standpoint, but then also how to refine my instructional moves in the classroom and even my design of college level lessons and the implementation."[61]

In discussion about Gay's influence on her scholar identity, like others, Gay had a significant impact on Carter Andrews' scholar iden- tity. She revealed that she tries to embody and act culturally responsive and relevant to the needs of the people she is serving:

> It really pushed me to think about the difference between relevance and responsiveness, and how as a scholar, my own research program, my public profile, my practi- tioner work is both relevant to the context and the issues at hand in education at any given time. This is why I was so glad to have found it (culturally responsive teaching). And now as I'm talking to you, I'm thinking I came upon Gay after Gloria Ladson-Billings, what culturally relevant pedagogy was about and culturally relevant teaching. But then, Geneva's work really ele- vated and articulated responsiveness and how relevance and responsiveness are both important. So as a scholar,

---

61 Ibid.

*I actually try to remember to be both and try to model that. How am I both relevant to my students and responsive as a leader, right? As a scholar who is also an administrator, how am I relevant in my leadership and how is my leadership culturally responsive to the needs of the people that I'm both serving and in community with? So I really do try to embody and enact those dimensions that Gay outlines.*[62]

It is important to take this moment to point out something that arose in all the interviews. Gloria Ladson-Billings and her idea of culturally relevant pedagogy was consistently coupled with culturally responsive teaching. We authors also agreed with that coupling, almost as though there is the unstated question of how can you speak of one without speaking of the other? They are literally two sides of the same coin, a coin minted in the mission of creating pedagogies and practices that support the humanization of historically marginalized students and sparking their genius. It is a pure editorial decision to not go into the work of Ladson-Billings here, but we have no doubt that her work is equally foundational and inspiring. However, this particular work is focused on Geneva Gay's work and contributions.

Carter Andrews framed Geneva Gay's work as a celebration of various aspects of identity, not just racial identity, but multiple identities in teaching and learning to counter today's hostile political climate:

*[Her work] doesn't negate dominance or privilege in one area, but her work does give us ways forward to both critique power and privilege and simultaneously celebrate our generality. I think her work supports Beverly Daniel Tatum—the argument that we are simultaneously dominant and subordinate. So what Geneva's work does is it doesn't shy away from the critique of power and privilege, but it really does center affirmation and celebration of difference—in a way that's still nuanced and critical.*

62 Ibid.

*It's not like this surface level multiculturalism.*[63]

When speaking about the importance of Geneva Gay being a Black woman in the field of education, Carter Andrews pointed out how Black women educators bring an ontological standpoint to theorizing culture, conceptualizing culture that people of other identities cannot. "Even if she doesn't name it as Black feminist thought or practice, I believe her scholarship and intellectual work is informed by those ontological and epistemological standpoints. How she shows up in the world as a Black woman has so much to do with how she even conceptualized culturally responsiveness, her lived experiences as a Black woman in a certain time and certain place inform that."

To close, Carter Andrews went on to elucidate the different lenses Geneva Gay brings to her work as a Black woman:

> *I think that's very important because what it does is it not only allows her to bring a racialized lens, but a raced-gendered lens. That intersectional standpoint is important for thinking about responsiveness because we know young people have intersectional identities, multiplicative identities, right? So the unconscious and conscious ways that Dr. Gay draws from her multiplicative identities in her writing and theorizing and conceptualizing are such beautiful gifts to the total package.*[64]

## David Stovall

David Stovall is a professor in the departments of Black Studies and Criminology, Law & Justice at the University of Illinois at Chicago. His scholarship investigates Critical Race Theory, the relationship between housing and education, and the intersection of race, place and school. In the attempt to bring theory to action, he works with community organizations and schools to address issues of equity,

---

63 Ibid.
64 Ibid.

justice and abolishing the school/prison nexus.[65]

Stovall described his first encounters with Geneva Gay's work in the year 2000 at an American Educational Research Association (AERA) meeting where he saw her speak. He characterized Geneva Gay as "more forward thinking and still kind of tied to the radical tradition of where multicultural education research originated."[66]

When asked about how his interactions with Geneva Gay influenced his career and professional choices, Stovall spoke to the rootedness of Geneva Gay's work. "All movements can become co-opted. All intellectual spaces of critique and possibility can be co-opted, but for me her work serves as the reminder to hold true to what it is that you are trying to do, and it of course will take other iterations, but this thing around remembering your foundation of work and then saying O.K., based on the foundation, here's what I may have. I always get a sense of rootedness in her work, and that's the kind of thing that I try to do with my own work."[67]

When speaking about Geneva Gay's influence on his scholar identity, Stovall reminisced about a play Gay engaged in with her students at AERA and how this opened up an important space for him to do his work:

> *They were putting forward their own counter-stories and how they started to develop culturally responsive practices and then the realities of doing that work in schools where there weren't a lot of resources. So it was telling me that she's thinking about this in ways that aren't necessarily lifted up by the academy. And for me that's a very important space. I do not look to the academy for any type of validation, right? I am much more concerned about what this means for young folks and families in a real world who are going through things and are*

65 "David Stovall," University of Illinois at Chicago, accessed September 21, 2022, https://blst.uic.edu/profiles/stovall-david/.
66 David Stovall (Professor of Black Studies and Criminology, Law & Justice) in discussion with the author, September, 2022.
67 Ibid.

*experiencing white supremacy in a form of marginaliza-*
*tion and isolation in all.* [68]

Stovall reflected on the prophetic nature of Geneva Gay's research in light of today's hostile political climate, he stated that Geneva Gay, along with Derrick Bell (the "father" of critical race theory) told us legislation like this was coming and that "Gay was always saying, 'Look, you can't rest on the laurels of the small victory, you have to understand that you are operating under white supremacy. If you're in a schoolhouse, you have to understand that you're often operating behind enemy lines.'"[69] Stovall continued to expound on what Geneva Gay meant by this. "You will experience certain forms of duress in that space (schools), and you have to be willing to work with others, understanding that it will take something else for you to do revolutionary work behind enemy lines."[70]

When envisioning the role of culturally responsive teaching and its' role continuing into the 21st century, Stovall discussed how Geneva Gay challenged people's understanding of the theory and how they make connections with their students.

> *Geneva changed the language. I think she changed the language, and she changed the language in a way that was pressing people to put race, class, gender, age, ability and sexual orientation into not only their lexicon, but into their understanding, right? I think that it is often so interesting because when I've seen her check, folks, and say, "Look, don't get it twisted. Don't misread what is written." This is a call to work, and it is a call to challenge yourself, right? So I think though, the future and present of culturally responsive teaching is really saying, look, if you're not clear about who you are, who your students are, and where there might be disconnects, and*

---

68 Ibid.
69 Ibid.
70 Ibid.

*how are you working to make connections.*[71]

Stovall also framed the role of culturally responsive teaching in the 21st century as a movement that centers around relationships with people.

I think that is what moves folks in the future, is that reminder, right? This is about movement work–resistance work, protest work. Revolutionary configurations are about being in relationship with people, right? So if you are trying to build something, you have to be in relationship with folks to understand what it is that you're trying to build, and I think that's a lasting presence of Gay's work.

When contributing his thoughts about the importance of Gay's legacy as a Black woman in educational thought and practice, Stovall framed Gay's stance as having two different meanings for Black excellence in education.

> *It's critical because she stands in the face of two things. One is the current demographics of teaching in the United States, being 80% white and female. And the second, as a Black woman, reminding folks of who are the keepers of relationship building, who are the keepers of actually building positive communities with students, particularly students of color, particularly Black students and how she always would put herself in the long historical trajectory of Black women teachers, right?*[72]

Stovall continued to expand on Gay's place in the long historical trajectory of Black women teachers and her contributions to Black youth:

> *I think that is key because it's a reminder of who actually held the history, story, culture, and who communicated that with Black youth in times where they were more reminded of their disposability than of their humanity, right? Gay is unwavering around her position and*

---

71 Ibid.
72 Ibid.

*understanding as a Black woman and how she's con-*
*nected to that history of educators who refused white*
*supremacy.*[73]

## Gholdy Muhammad

Gholdy Muhammad is an Associate Professor of Literacy, Language, and Culture in the College of Education at the University of Illinois at Chicago. She studies Black historical excellence within educational communities with goals of reframing curriculum and instruction today. Muhammad's scholarship has appeared in leading academic journals and books, including Research in the Teaching of English, Urban Education, Journal of Adolescent and Adult Literacy, Language Arts, and Written Communication.[74] Most recently, her book, *Cultivating Genius: An Equity Framework for Culturally and Historically Responsive Literacy*, has become one of the most interesting texts in multicultural education.[75]

When asked about Geneva Gay's influence on her career and professional choices, Muhammad reminisced about the word responsive and discussed the responsibility we have to the needs in our schools:

> *This idea of like, how do we start with Blackness and*
> *teaching Black children better as that was my focus. That*
> *was like what I wanted to be known for in the work I*
> *wanted to put out in the world. I loved Geneva Gay. I*
> *remember really spending time on just the word respon-*
> *sive because I think that's what she named this idea of*
> *responsiveness, and the responsibility we have. And not*
> *just being responsive to the students' lives, their culture,*
> *their race, their identities, but also being responsive to*
> *the times and the needs of the times in our schools and*

73 Ibid.
74 "Gholdy E. Muhammad," University of Illinois at Chicago, accessed September 17, 2022, https://education.uic.edu/profiles/muhammad-gholnecsar/.
75 Gholdy Muhammad, *Cultivating Genius: An Equity Framework for Culturally and Historically Responsive Literacy* (New York: Scholastic Teaching Resources, 2020).

*from their foundations. It just has really stuck with me.*[76]

Muhammad said that if it was not for the foundational work of Geneva Gay, she would not have been able to build her own work into literacy and curriculum and instruction. Muhammad spoke about "how [Gay] would write about how to use students' excellencies, the things that they know, who they are, their knowledges, their resources, the things that they have learned in the world and how to use all different parts of who they are to teach them more excellently."[77]

She further illuminated the impact Gay's ideas had on her career. "I began, along with other scholars, like cultural scholars, who really took this idea of looking at children's identities and histories and language and all these things as resources to build upon. I started to engage in my own research and go a little further back right into different parts of Black history or American history too, and look at how Black people organize, look at how they read, and I focused on literacy, more so."[78]

When asked about Gay's work as a counter to anti-critical race theory legislative efforts, Muhammad explained that the politicians lack an understanding of educational theory and practice. "They are finding new and different ways to ban anything excellent around Blackness around Black children. I don't think they ever really understand pedagogy and theory, but they do understand the disdain and the hate for Black people."[79] She continued to elaborate on the anti-Black messages this wave of legislation that bans critical race theory promotes, "I really do feel now this is not really about anti-critical race theory as much as it is anti- Black, anti-Black excellence, anti-Black thought, anti-Black liberation, anti-Black people."[80] Countering this wave of legislation, Muhammad pointed out the central focus of Gay's work that inspires excellence in education for all children:

76 Gholdy E. Muhammad (Associate Professor of Literacy, Language, and Culture) in discussion with author, September, 2022.
77 Ibid.
78 Ibid.
79 Ibid.
80 Ibid.

*At the foundation of her work are all those things–black*
*liberation, black thought, and she's really writing in a*
*way that is good for all children, not just Black children.*
*I feel that if [politicians] really read the work around*
*multicultural education, anti-bias education, which is*
*all kind of censored and hinged upon, like the work that*
*she's put out, they would not live or swim in pools of*
*ignorance."[81]*

Muhammad pivoted the conversation to the importance of Gay being a Black woman in the field. She spoke to how Gay is continuing a rich legacy in education:

*I just feel like when it comes to culturally responsive*
*education and cultural responsiveness, and I'm talking*
*about before any of our times, Black women, since the*
*early 19th century, have been the forerunners, not just*
*in culturally responsive education, but in education, in*
*the improvement of education, the excellence of educa-*
*tion. I think she's continuing a rich legacy. You know of*
*people like Maria Stewart, Elizabeth Flood, Anna Julia*
*Cooper, Mary McLeod Bethune, Clare Mohammed …*
*she builds upon this legacy of Black women. And as a*
*Black woman, she has a unique positionality.[82]*

But for Muhammad, Geneva Gay being a Black woman and taking the work of the ideas of her foremothers while navigating the torrents of being a Black woman in higher education, was most powerful and inspirational:

*She builds upon this legacy of black women. And as*
*a black woman, she has a unique position. We have*
*experiences and identities in multiple intersections,*
*even when you think about just race, class. And that's*
*a unique stance and perspective of the world. When you*

81 Ibid.
82 Ibid.

*have lived that way and when the world has treated you that way, and when you've had to react, respond, resist, recoup (said with a defiant chuckle), reclaim your life when the world is kind of coming at you like that, right? And so that means that you got something powerful to say, and the world should be listening to black women. And so now she's coming from this as a black woman doing this research, so she's coming from all of that, and that's what I think makes the work so special.*[83]

Within the struggle Muhammad describes one of the most inspirational aspects of Gay's work, something others were also pointing out, Gay's work emanates from a space of love and respect for the humanity of others, of children, of students.

## Conclusion

There can be no doubt that the work of Geneva Gay has been crucial to education. As our noted scholars have pointed out, the power of the notion of culturally responsive teaching is one of the most valuable influences on the work of scholars, researchers, and educators who are dedicated to promoting equitable, empowering practices for children and youths. From a contemporary like Christine Sleeter to a newer scholar in the game like Gholdy Muhammad, the profound impact of Geneva Gay – not only her ideas but also her presence – is indispensable, unavoidable, revolutionary, and wholly human.

As David Kirkland declared, "It's time we give her flowers,"[84] and he is absolutely on point with that sentiment. Or as Christine Sleeter said, "I've seen every once in a while, (Gay) not getting the credit that she deserves, and so I'm glad you're doing this."[85] Or, as Dorinda Carter Andrews said, "I'm glad she's still with us, you know, so many of our seminal intellects have transitioned to be with the ancestors, particularly our Black intellectuals. I am glad that Geneva is still with

83 Ibid.
84 Kirkland, interview.
85 Sleeter, interview.

us, that we still have opportunities to learn with and from her."[86] Or as David Stovall said, "I think the most important thing is that she is as towering a figure as she is, she also reminds folks of their responsibility in doing this work right. So if you are talking about educating in any way that's critical, it's culturally responsive. There is a duty and responsibility to your community to get this right. Right? And I think that is what I pull from her work."[87]

What is a testament to the power and impact of an idea? The fact that so many of us attempt to practice culturally responsive teaching before we even read the book or know her name is profound. Geneva Gay didn't kick in the door to make inroads for a brilliant idea and the embrace of students who are historically marginalized. No. Geneva Gay blew up the institution, and as the dust settled, she emerged as one of the key figures that changed education. Changed education. It reminds us of people like Miles Davis, Spike Lee, Toni Morrison, and Jimi Hendrix, artists who *changed* the fundamental ways in which people thought about an art and craft. Geneva Gay stands in that pantheon of people who mastered and then went on to fundamentally change the ways in which that art or craft is produced and theorized. Geneva Gay had, ultimately, a powerful hand in pushing educators to be responsive to the cultures and needs of students.

The humanity in Gay's work is ever-present and clear. She is encouraging us to see the humanity, the uniqueness, the brilliance of all our children and those under our charge in a classroom. For centuries, American education has exercised systemically and institutionally oppressive practices on African American, Latino, Asian American, and Native American students, and there are far too many examples to mention for that to be an invalid or misguided statement. A part of that oppression is evident in the persistent school-based trends of the criminalization of Black bodies, consistently lowered expectations, a slowly changing curriculum that embraces the full humanity and

---

86 Carter Andrews, interview.
87 Stovall, interview.

beauty of all, lack of accurate and honest inclusion of histories, suspicion and fear of children, the inability to connect on a substantive level with students who are historically marginalized, and a resistance to embracing and centering their cultures in the classroom. We can thank Geneva Gay for creating an idea and method that promotes the humanity of not just students who are marginalized, but all students.

Before we go, thanks to Christine Sleeter, David Kirkland, Dorinda Carter Andrews, David Stovall, and Gholdy Muhammad. Their thoughts and reflections were a sincere joy to capture. But, the mic is going back to Gholdy Muhammad to close this out. As the interview was ending, she added this, a sentiment that encapsulates the point and spirit of this book:

> We need these kinds of moments where we take on, when we say, you know, she requires our specificity at this time, you know, in her work. And I think just by honoring and saying that it's really important for her, for other Black women too. And to really build this thing up and to be supported. You know, because I cannot imagine she's had it easy at institutions, doing this work, during the time she did it, in institutions that are mostly white. I can't imagine it's easy (chuckle). So you know, what does it take to keep that idea of joy and sustainability while you're doing that? That's really important to ask and to figure out. It's something that I'm also asking and trying to figure out too.[88]

Finally, thank you Dr. Geneva Gay, for the power in your ideas and the power in you.

---

88 Muhammad, interview.

# Part II

The Transformation of Teaching Theory Using Culturally Responsive Teaching

# CHAPTER 3

# The Growth of Culturally Responsive Teaching in Teaching Methodologies

*By Sarah Militz-Frielink & Regina Lewis*

We (Sarah Militz-Frielink and Regina A. Lewis) dedicate this chapter to the legacy of Dr. Geneva Gay and the indelible shaping influences that her scholarship has had on our work. We follow Gay in believing that all children can succeed, and we follow her precepts about "achievement," which include that culture counts, conventional reform is inadequate, intention without action is insufficient, cultural diversity is full of strength and vitality, competence or incompetence is never universal or all-inclusive, and test scores and grades are symptoms, not causes of achievement problems.[89] We further align ourselves with Gay's explanation of culturally responsive teaching, which "validates, facilitates, liberates, and empowers ethnically diverse students by simultaneously cultivating their cultural integrity, individual abilities, and academic success."[90]

In what follows, the two of us (Militz-Frielink and Lewis) conduct a dialogue about culturally responsive teaching and weigh the influences that Gay's theories have had on our scholarship and teaching in higher education. We focus specifically on Gay's innovative research

89 Gay Geneva, *Culturally Responsive Teaching: Theory, Research, and Practice* (New York, Teachers College Press, 2018).
90 Ibid, 53.

agenda that highlights her unique contributions to educational policy reform and to the need to promote critical forms of multiculturalism. We intend this dialogue to showcase the essential features of her work and how it has impacted both our classrooms and scholarship—making culturally responsive teaching a tangible reality not only for us, but for countless others nationwide.

However, in order to provide some necessary background for better understanding both Gay's legacy and the upcoming dialogue, we need first to discuss some of the essential features of Gay's educational thought. We hope that this approach—first outlining the contours of Gay's thought, followed by our dialogue-- will clarify how we came to be beneficiaries of, and heirs to, Gay's moral and intellectual legacy.

Prior to beginning this project last year, Militz-Frielink conducted research with graduate students who are culturally, linguistically, and ethnically diverse. For example, in her recent book, she examined the phenomenon *transnational endarkened feminist epistemology,* (hereafter EFE*),* where she interviewed students who had undertaken a study abroad program with Cynthia B. Dillard in Ghana (in conjunction with the University of Georgia, Athens).[91] This research demonstrates the myriad ways in which Dillard, the intellectual architect of EFE, actualized this teaching/research paradigm in her classroom, and how her students experienced and made meaning of their diasporic-oriented foreign study in Ghana. Through classroom observations, interviews with Dillard, and dialogues with Dillard's students, Militz-Frielink's study attempted to identify EFE's origins and the ways in which this paradigm helped students make meaning out of their respective experiences. The students' meaning-making experiences included a host of additional themes that emanated from the EFE paradigm, such as healing from past trauma, identity development, cultural histories, and non-religious spirituality. The study concludes with a discussion of the educational policy implications of EFE and

---

91 Sarah Militz-Frielink, *Liberation in Higher Education: A White Researcher's Journey Through the Shadows* (New York: Peter Lang, 2019).

with Militz-Frielink's recommendations for practitioners, especially white practitioners in higher education who work with students who are culturally, linguistically, and/or ethnically diverse. Militz-Frielink has always tried to be conscious about the need to incorporate culturally responsive teaching in her classroom, whether she was teaching special education or philosophy of education. Gay offers a concise definition of this vital moral ideal:

> *Culturally responsive teaching is defined as using the cultural characteristics, experiences, and perspectives of ethnically diverse students as conduits for teaching them more effectively. It is based on the assumption that when academic knowledge and skills are situated within the lived experiences and frames of reference of students, they are more personally meaningful, have higher interest appeal, and are learned more easily and thoroughly.*[92]

Prior to beginning this Geneva Gay book project, Regina Lewis created cultural competence training to address the needs and issues schools and organizations are challenged with concerning equity, diversity, and inclusion. Her CEID program – Cultural Excellence: Ideas and Discussions is an award-winning equity, diversity, and inclusion training program that has been recognized for its "nonprescriptive" "all inclusive" "data driven" and "action oriented" approach to this work. Additionally, this program provides tools to engage in meaningful conversations, building blocks for systemic culturally identified groups, equity, diversity, and transformational shifts. Whether in her trainings or in the classroom, Lewis has taken the tenants of Gay's culturally responsive work to help others to embrace their cultural mindset (one's own perspective) while making a cultural mind shift (understanding and being open to learning other's perspectives).

---

92 Gay Geneva, "Preparing for Culturally Responsive Teaching," *Journal of Teacher Education 53* no. 2, (March/April 2002): 106. https://www.cwu.edu/teaching-learning/sites/cts.cwu.edu.teaching-learning/files/documents/PreparingforCulturallyResponsiveTeaching,%20Geneva%20Gay.pdf.

During the COVID-19 pandemic, schools had to quickly shift from physical presence in the classroom to online modalities. Not only did instructors have to learn how to teach students who do not prefer online instruction and create a remote style of teaching, but also how to be culturally responsive simultaneously. This involved the whole student, which included their family dynamic, socioeconomics, access, ability, and support. Lewis co-authored a journal article which focused on culturally responsive online instruction and remote learning. For many, what seemed new and not complex, became necessary and relevant. For instance, teaching how to create backgrounds or blurred background to provide privacy for students, walking students through how to place their names below their video to create a sense of belonging. Cameras on were encouraged, but not mandatory to build community. Furthermore, breakout rooms became a space not only for group work, but to have private conversations. Once classes were physically reopened, as department chair, I offered flexible modalities to accommodate diverse needs of students. This included what is referred to as hyflex, which allows students to have the ability to come to the physical classroom space or join the class virtually from anywhere they have access to the internet.

Many of these techniques responded to the normative idea that culturally responsive teaching must be "multidimensional" in nature; such as Gay's educational theory that "Multidimensional culturally responsive teaching encompasses curriculum content, learning context, classroom climate, student-teacher relationships, instructional techniques, classroom management, and performance assessment."[93] In other words, Gay wants us to be alert to the complicated layers of teacher awareness that comprise hospitable and intellectual classroom environments [whether in the physical space or virtually online}.

Prior to beginning this book project, Lewis has led and has forged alliances with worldwide organizations, specializing in leadership development and organizational communication. With clients

93 Geneva Gay, *Culturally Responsive Teaching*, 39.

ranging from Fortune 500 companies through not-for-profit agencies to educational institutions, Lewis' intellectual versatility is reflected in a wide range of activities she has engaged in over the years. Her work as a multicultural consulting partner, international speaker, virtual moderator and entrepreneur—CEO of ReginaSpeaking, LLC, has enabled her to serve clients in Saudi Arabia, Lebanon, Hong Kong, China, Ethiopia, Vietnam, Brazil, and the United States to name a few.

As a war veteran who previously served in the United States Air Force, Lewis is currently the Special Assistant to the President for Academic Excellence and Inclusion, Department Chair and Professor of Communication at Pikes Peak Community College, while also finding time to serve as an executive coach for the Center for Creative Leadership. Regina has always sought to implement forms of culturally responsive teaching in her classroom.

Culturally responsive teaching, for Gay, is also humanistic at its core. "While its primary constituency is individuals and groups whose humanity has been, and often still is, denigrated by mainstream peoples, politics, and practices, others are considered benefactors as well. This means that culturally responsive teaching has value for majority and minority students, for both similar and different reasons, and that these benefits are direct and indirect, individually and collectively."[94] Despite the geographic distance in our respective locations, we have designed similar multicultural classroom environments. Our students from diverse backgrounds include white students who also benefit enormously from culturally responsive teaching. Culturally responsive teaching is normative and ethical. Geneva Gay writes:

> *Educational discourse about equity and social justice recommends extending similar rights and opportunities from other ethnic groups especially those discriminated against, oppressed, and marginalized (that is, minority groups of color). They deserve parallel rights*

94 Geneva Gay, *Culturally Responsive Teaching*, 44.

*and opportunities like those received by majority groups of students. Since culture and education are inseparably linked, and different ethnic groups have different cultures, it is both the normal and right thing to do to incorporate cultural diversity into educative processes intended for ethnically, racially, and socially diverse students.*[95]

Once again, echoing Gay's stance, we attempt to champion issues of racial equity and social justice in the classroom. We believe that culturally responsive teaching should be a right for everyone who enters our classrooms, not to mention a right for those millions of other Americans who are not afforded equality of educational opportunity.

Yet another key tenet of Gay's thought is that the power of culturally responsive *caring* is immense. "Caring is one of those things that most educators agree is important in working effectively with students, but they are hard-pressed to characterize it in actual practice, or to put a functional face on it that goes beyond feelings of empathy and emotional attachment."[96] As we hope to discuss in the pages ahead, both of us seek to embody culturally responsive caring, a kind of caring which "focuses on caring *for* instead of *about* the personal well-being and academic success of ethnically diverse students, with a clear understanding that the two are interrelated."[97]

When it comes to the spoken word, Geneva Gay emphasizes how culture is an important variable, which affects the quality of how teachers and students communicate with each other.[98] Teachers often assume there is only one way to communicate across "all circumstances, audiences, and contexts."[99] However, this is certainly not one of the assumptions that we utilize in our classrooms! We attempt to improve each of our intercultural interactions through including

---

95 Geneva Gay, *Culturally Responsive Teaching*, 45
96 Ibid, 58.
97 Ibid.
98 Ibid.
99 Ibid, 91.

different discourse styles with our students of color to make connections with and throughout our conversations.

We encourage different written and spoken expressions to increase student achievement in our classrooms. According to Geneva Gay, there are two techniques for organizing written and spoken expressions: topic-centered and topic-associative or topic-chaining.[100] European-Americans prefer the first, while Latino-Americans, African American, Native Americans, and Native Hawaiians prefer the second.[101]

> *In topic-centered discourse speakers focus on one issue at a time; arrange facts and ideas in logical, linear order; and make explicit referential, temporal, and spatial relationships…A topic associative style of talking and writing also has been called topic-chaining, performance discourse, and narrative style. It is episodic, anecdotal, thematic, and integrative.[102]*

We value the different techniques students use to speak and write in our classrooms. For instance, Militz-Frielink frequently incorporates journal assignments to encourage students to use their topic associative styles in writing, which is important for students of color. Students who prefer topic-centered discourse can benefit from journaling as well. Lewis implements similar techniques through her discussions with students.

Geneva Gay highlights the importance of being conscious of the cultural codes and cues we use in regular communication with our students, including proverbs, parables, colloquialisms, and educational jargon. Both of us strive to "decode, translate, and interpret these codes for culturally diverse students."[103]

Inspired by Gay's legacies, we both recruit from a range of resources to enable students from diverse backgrounds to feel comfortable. We

---

100 Ibid.
101 Ibid.
102 Ibid., 124.
103 Ibid, 140.

use "books, articles, films, music, audio recordings, and a variety of other resources from the internet that explain and visualize examples of different ethnic groups' culture and communication."[104]

Geneva Gay has emphasized how important it is to have books that are free from bias and negative portrayals of ethnic groups.[105] Students can become "insulted, embarrassed, ashamed, and angered when reading and hearing negative portrayals of their ethnic groups or not hearing anything at all."[106] We have made an effort to include authors of color and authors who are social justice advocates in our curriculum for our students. Our students are excited when people who look like them are included in the curriculum.

We follow Geneva Gay's recommended learning styles for our diverse students of color in that we infuse these learning styles into our teaching and communicative patterns with students. The different dimensions we incorporate into our teaching include the procedural, communicative, substantive, environmental, organizational, perceptual, relational, and motivational.[107] Different students exhibit "purer" learning style characteristics than others.[108] For example, "highly ethnically affiliated African Americans will exhibit strong preferences for "group-ness" across procedural, motivational, relational, and substantive dimensions of learning because of the values their culture places on working collaboratively to accomplish tasks, emotionalism, and informal social interactions."[109] Middle class European Americans will prefer independence and self-initiation.[110] Japanese and Chinese American students will exhibit more bi-stylistic dimensions of learning styles due to the focus their culture places on familial obligations and harmonious relationships.[111]

We identify the need for additional assistance and understanding

---

104 Ibid., 141.
105 Ibid.
106 Ibid., 151.
107 Ibid.
108 Ibid.
109 Ibid., 209
110 Ibid.
111 Ibid.

of the learning styles of students of color and we center our practice on various sensory modalities to ascertain which ones work best for our students. Our practice is constantly revising itself to include more models our students can experience in the classroom.

Geneva Gay discusses the importance of incorporating cooperative learning groups into the classroom, which studies show lead to "greater reasoning and clarity of expression in writing and reading as well as higher scores on school district writing proficiency tests."[112] We "build ethnic, racial, gender, social, and ability diversity into the organization and task assignments of groups"[113] and use multidimensional tasks and learning style preferences in the groups. Our students engage in small group discussions and creative projects during group time.

Finally, Gay emphasized the importance of communication as dynamic and complex in culturally relevant teaching. "In fact, it is the ultimate test! Because of its dynamic nature, teachers need to continually monitor their own communication habits and learn about those of other ethnic and cultural groups."[114] In recognizing that dialogue, at its best, also reflects an essential improvisational element, we would like to salute Gay for her ultimate teaching wisdom-- that "authentic teaching means venturing into uncertainty" and thus one must be receptive to improvising in every phase of the educational project. Now, onto the dialogue…

## Dialogue about Culturally Responsive Teaching

**Sarah Militz-Frielink:** I focus on holistic and integrated learning for my students where I teach personal, moral, social, political, cultural and academic knowledge and skills simultaneously. My teaching includes discussion boards and journal entries where students build on their personal experiences and respond to each other. Their responses to each other on the discussion boards builds a better community of

112 Ibid., 218.
113 Ibid., 227.
114 Ibid., 140.

diverse learners.

**Regina Lewis:** It is important that each person believes they have something of value to offer. I like to place this in the context of diversity. Beyond representation, what do they each bring to the table that enhances the experience? For example, a person's race maybe considered Black or African American, but in addition, I have them illuminate their intersections that make up who they are culturally. Additionally, I invite different perspectives and I do not operate from majority rules. Instead, we work to collaborate on ideas and discussions.

**Sarah Militz-Frielink:** I make sure that all of my curriculum focuses on different ethnic groups and authors of color, so students experience different voices and points of view. My readings are from a diverse group of authors, which helps students connect to people who are like them or people who are different from them. This helps my white students recognize and start to understand white supremacy and how it works in the United States when they read diverse perspectives on racial justice and diversity. This helps my students of color connect more deeply with classroom materials knowing that people who look like them are writing the materials we are using. I also focus on the accomplishments of people of color and their contributions to the progress of this country.

**Regina Lewis:** I immediately welcome students into my class and state that I welcome all pronouns and cultures. Additionally, I provide students a document with a series of questions to help guide them in sharing their cultural background. I ask questions such as family dynamic, educational experience, music and food they enjoy, how to pronounce their names. I also ask what I can do to make them feel valued and what do they need from me to be successful in my class. I offer different options to complete or understand assignments. These options are given to every student. I organically incorporate different representations of cultures without deficit. Whether it is in imagery, text, socially, or exercises.

I use apps such as Forvo, which is an app that teaches how to pronounce names.

**Sarah Militz-Frielink:** We celebrate different ethnic group's cultural values, traditions, communication, learning styles, contributions, and relational patterns through discussion and debriefing in the classroom about these aspects of diversity. My students know that I am not afraid to discuss racism and race in the United States and that different cultures play a huge role in our conversations as well. The readings by diverse authors enhance our discussions, and I bring up topics such as the school-to-prison pipeline, the criminal justice system, Black Lives Matter, the environment, and LGBTQ issues to name a few. We focus on critiquing social issues that affect people of color and different social groups.

**Regina Lewis:** I invite different perspectives and do not operate from majority rules. I use VARKing in my teaching style to address at least four of the learning styles. I invite students to share how they learn best and share different learning techniques. I constantly share quotes and excepts from Geneva Gay's work and Carter G. Woodson's work to help place educational experiences and challenges in perspective. I have students work in groups and dyads to learn from one another.

**Sarah Militz-Frielink:** I incorporate cultural humility and self-reflection in all of my communications with students and community members. Students are encouraged to use their own voice in their creative projects and draw upon their culture or learn about people from other cultures for the projects we are completing in class.

**Regina Lewis:** In all of my classes, I have students present a project from their culture, learn and present a culture different from their own, and I intentionally find people from different cultures who are contributors to the work I am teaching. Other times, I explain concepts using diverse figures. For instance, if I am explaining physics, I may show a Black athlete diving off a diving board. I do not point out the person's race, I just organically incorporate the race into the discussion.

**Sarah Militz-Frielink:** We critique mass media and use critical theory to analyze media from the perspective of gender, race, and social class. We watch films in class and discuss magazines, television, newspapers and mass media from a critical theoretical perspective. This way my students are learning about the morals and values, which are sometimes pejorative that this societal curriculum portrays. I strive to teach my students to critique media and to not believe what they see and read right away. This gives them knowledge, which is power to discern between messages that disempower them as people of color and empower them as people of color.

**Regina Lewis:** I bring in different perspectives and we discuss the differences. I also help students think critically by having them bring in articles and other forms of research and I compare their research with factually accurate primary sources. I teach the students how to analyze, text, music, and video using primary and secondary sources.

**Sarah Militz-Frielink:** I contextualize issues within race, class, ethnicity, gender, including multiple kinds of knowledge and perspectives in my teaching through meaningful conversations about these issues where I encourage students to think critically about these issues and analyze them from a position of equity, freedom and justice.

**Regina Lewis:** I explain the importance of diversity in our work and the contributions of different cultures of this work. Additionally, I provide reading materials, videos, speeches, etc. that are presented by different cultural groups.

**Sarah Militz-Frielink:** I connect with my students and encourage them to share their personal experiences in their writing with me. I give them positive feedback and encouragement to be the best students they can be. I am compassionate when any issue arises in the classroom with a student who may have a problem and who is in need of help. I offer my assistance to students who need extra help with class work.

**Regina Lewis:** Images, music, food, conversations, experiences.

All of these are areas of opportunity that I have taken advantage of to symbolize culture and expand student knowledge. I also share personal stories from my cultural experiences to help deepen student understanding.

**Sarah Militz-Frielink:** I encourage my undergraduate students to go to graduate school or pursue whatever dreams they may have post-graduation. I offer to write them letters of recommendation to boost their academic careers. I also encourage them to go to academic conferences when possible and publish their writing. I incorporate mentorship in my practice as an academic to inspire students to achieve their goals and create new aspirations.

**Regina Lewis:** I invite all perspectives and ideas. I speak to the historical and current challenges of race, class, ethnicity, and gender without singling out anyone. This is for the purpose of building community and empathy.

**Sarah Militz-Frielink:** I facilitate a culture of caring in my classroom. I invite all my students into a conversation and encourage students to question and dialogue with each other. I confirm each student as a participant with full knowledge of the subject. I tell students we are in the process of remembering what we already know through the dialogue and questioning. I believe as Carter G. Woodson professed in sparking the genius in every student.

**Regina Lewis:** I learn students' names and how to pronounce them immediately. I use their names in all of my correspondence with them and in any interaction. I work hard to see and understand how my students individually relate to their experiences. I then reach them from that place. This includes code switching on my part. I have built relationships of mutual respect outside of my culture to learn and understand the cultural nuances of other cultures. I use this information to meet students where their needs are.

**Sarah Militz-Frielink:** Dr. Gay has inspired my teaching to include culturally responsive teaching as part of the foundation of my philosophy of education.

**Regina Lewis:** I am a professor of communication. Understanding the work of Dr. Gay has enhanced my way of teaching and reaching my scholars. I have also found that my business, ReginaSpeaking, LLC has reached further and deeper because more people know that my talks and trainings will include them.

**Sarah Militz-Frielink:** Dr. Gay has inspired my writing to focus on African American Studies and all areas involving social issues. My writing has also focused on race and racism in the United States. Dr. Gay's influence on me has shaped my scholar identity to interact with all cultures.

**Regina Lewis:** I struggled in my K-12 education and was led to believe it was me. Eventually, I learned that what I was experiencing was a lack of cultural responsiveness from my teachers. Fortunately, over time, I was inspired by culturally responsive teachers. This gave me the courage and drive to continue my education to the level of Ph.D.

# CHAPTER 4

# Different Does Not Mean Deficit: Teaching Adults with Disabilities Using Culturally Responsive Teaching Theory

*By Karina Avila*

Have you ever been in a crowd of people, and just felt different? I have. I have been in crowds of people and felt like people did not look like me, did not talk like me, were smarter than me, and much more. Throughout my undergraduate sojourn at Northern Illinois University (NIU), (1) I learned about leadership while reaching the highest cadet rank—NIU Cadet Battalion Commander (CBC) in ROTC (The first female CBC) and (2) As a participant in the NIU Undergraduate Research Program, I learned how to conduct academic research. Specifically, I learned how to inspire people using research theories such as leadership and culturally responsive teaching. Subsequently, I applied those theories in two distinctively different careers—(1) Active-Duty, U.S. Army Officer / Captain and (2) Qualified Intellectual Disabilities Professional (QIDP).

Currently, I am a QIDP in the state of Illinois and I use the research theory—culturally responsive teaching that I learned at NIU. Dr. Geneva Gay the architect of culturally responsive teaching once said, "different does not mean deficit." As an undergraduate, I internalized her words and that significantly changed the trajectory of my life experiences and careers. I am Hispanic American and I speak Spanish fluently. I was nurtured in a bilingual home by parents who migrated from Mexico and English was their second language. Growing up, I struggled to understand why I had to work so hard to fit in my Hispanic culture while also focusing to be successful in the United States. As Abraham Quintanilla said in the Selena movie, "We have to be more Mexican than the Mexicans and more American than the Americans, both at the same time! It's exhausting!" This is how I felt all of my life. Different. In school, teachers never saw that.

I learned from Dr. Gay, that everything that distinguishes one differently than others is what makes us unique. People respond well when they feel accepted in all forms. In this case, I continue to use the teaching strategies of Geneva Gay who believes in critical cultural consciousness of teachers, culturally pluralistic classroom climates, diverse communities of learners, and multicultural curriculum and instruction.[115] Geneva Gay writes about the importance of recognizing difference and diversity in the classroom. "To attempt to ignore diversity in the classroom, or pretend that it is not an important variable in teaching and learning, merely submerges rather than purges differences and demeans the humanity of ethnically and culturally diverse students."[116] I did not have teachers who were Hispanic and I did not have teachers who spoke Spanish. I was always different, but at the same time, I knew there was nothing wrong with me.

## Working with People who Have Disabilities

As I went through college, people with disabilities gained a special place in my heart. I began to see that they also felt different or looked different in a crowd of people, much like I felt all of my life. I wanted to be that change in their life to get them to see that different is okay.

---

115 Geneva Gay, "Culturally Responsive Teaching in Special Education for Ethnically Diverse Students: Setting the Stage," *Qualitative Studies in Education* 15, no. 6 (2002).
116 Ibid, 618.

I am now a Qualified Intellectual Disabilities Professional (QIDP) working as a Service Coordinator. "Service Coordinators fulfill a variety of roles—from advocate to educator to leader. They are resilient in the face of challenge. They are uncompromising in the provision of person directed supports."[117] To become a Service Coordinator, I completed the Developmental Disability Professional Certificate Program. The program included an application that required three professional letters of recommendation, a resume, and a background screening consent form.[118] In order to secure the position, I also needed to send in transcripts from my bachelor's degree program, write two essays, and show that I had one year of experience working with people who have developmental disabilities. After the application process, I had to complete all of the requirements of the Developmental Disability Professional (DDP) Certificate Program. These requirements included seven core training elements, which focused on topics such as supporting individuals with disabilities in the community and working with families.[119] In addition to core training, the DDP Certificate Program required three elective training classes. The curriculum in the electives covered aging and developmental disabilities; seizures; positioning, turning, and transferring; sexuality and developmental disabilities; promoting nutrition and wellness; job coaching; traumatic brain injury; history of sexual offense; leadership roles in human service agencies; community education and public relations; and autism.[120] I work with a caseload of about 50 people with disabilities. My mission is helping people with developmental delays and disabilities access better choices for life. I meet with my clients on a quarterly basis. The clients and I visit to talk about their life and what they want to accomplish.

## Dr. Geneva Gay's Influence on My Work

117 "NAQ Learn," Connect. Share, accessed August 22, 2022, https://www.qddp.org/about-the-program.
118 Ibid.
119 Ibid.
120 Ibid.

Dr. Gay believed that teachers' knowledge about and attitudes towards cultural diversity are powerful determinants of learning opportunities and outcomes for students who are ethnically and/or linguistically diverse. She believes in using student's "cultural orientations, background experiences, and ethnic identities as conduits to facilitate their teaching and learning."[121] I inspire my clients by using Dr. Gay's aforementioned teaching strategies. The more culturally empowered they are, the more they are willing to be open about their wants and needs.

**The R-Slur**

The R-word, which is also known as the R-slur is a mean-spirited term that still remains prevalent in today's society.[122] The Special Olympics organization expounds on the pejorative impact the R-word has on people with intellectual disabilities:

> *The R-word is a form of hate speech that stands for "retard," "retarded," or other offensive words ending in "-tard." While "mental retardation" was originally introduced as a medical term in 1961 for people with intellectual disabilities, in the decades since, the R-word has become an insult used all too commonly in everyday language. Those who use the R-word often do so with little regard for the pain it causes people with intellectual disabilities—and the exclusion it perpetuates in our society.[123]*

"Rosa's Law," which was signed by President Barack Obama in 2010 revised the term "mental retardation" to "intellectual disability" in U.S. federal law.[124] This law is key in promoting inclusion and

---

121 Geneva Gay, "Culturally Responsive Teaching in Special Education for Ethnically Diverse Students: Setting the Stage," 614.
122 "Why the R-word is the R-slur, Practice Inclusion: End the Use of the R-word," Special Olympics, accessed August 24, 2022, https://www.specialolympics.org/stories/impact/why-the-r-word-is-the-r-slur.
123 Ibid, para. 2.
124 Ibid.

acceptance for people with intellectual disabilities in their communities. This law is also pivotal in changing the way schools label groups of children who qualify for certain special education services.

## Speaking to People With Disabilities

Many people do not know how to bring up a conversation about people with disabilities. People fail to recognize ableism—a system of oppression that determines "who is valuable and worthy based on a person's language, appearance, religion, and/or their ability to satisfactorily [re]produce, excel, and behave."[125] Dis/ability is what people fail to realize. David Hernandez-Saca explains the meaning of dis/ability:

By dis/ability, I mean the sociocultural and political construction of the meanings of what it means to have a "disability." This is the social model of disability as opposed to a medical-psychological model of disability. The latter situates the "problem of disability" within my neurology, psychology, and emotions and in the need of "fixing," as opposed to the former understanding "dis/ability" as the social constructions of both "ability" and "disability": disability as an identity marker to be proud of, as well as to place pressure to (re)arrange society and its institutions, and to challenge its assumptions in order to view dis/ability as diversity and something natural.[126]

Anyone with a disability can do everything and anything anyone without a disability can do. Society needs to view disabilities from a different angle. Like Hernandez-Saca said, disability is something to be proud of and necessitates a change in society to view it as natural. For instance, people's bodies. Are they in a wheelchair and need to ensure a location that is wheelchair accessible? Their sensory habits. Do they prefer to be in a location that is silent versus loud? There are many factors that need to be considered; however, there is no disability that they need to "overcome". People are who they are, and

---

125 Talila A. Lewis, "January 2021 Working Definition of Ableism," January 1, 2021, accessed August 24, 2022, https://www.talilalewis.com/blog/january-2021-working-definition-of-ableism.
126 David I. Hernandez-Saca, "My Learning Dis/Ability and Disability Studies in Education Activism," *Peace Review* 31 no. 4 (2019): 489. doi:10.1080/10402659.2019.1800935.

anything in society can be adjusted.

Shurti Rajkumar discusses best practices when talking about disability.[127] He suggests centering disabled voices to avoid infantilization, recognizing that disability is a culture and identity—not a problem, doing research, and recognizing intersectionality.[128] Many journalists avoid speaking directly to the person with a disability when writing a story about disabilities and interview the parents or nondisabled people in an organization. This leads to further marginalization and infantilization of the person with the disability. Best practices recommend speaking directly to the person with the disability to adequately understand their lived experiences. The medical model of disability frames disability as a problem that must be corrected through medical intervention as opposed to viewing disability through a cultural form of identity. The social model of disability emphasizes the normalcy of disability and the need for society to accommodate. Doing research on ableist language and how to avoid using eugenics-based terms like "idiot" or "moron" is helpful for nondisabled people interested in taking the weight off people with disabilities to educate others about using nonharmful language.[129] It is important to recognize how people with disabilities can belong to multiple marginalized groups, which effect their everyday life experiences. For example, many of my clients have disabilities and simultaneously belong to a culturally, linguistically, and/or ethnically diverse group. This affects how they experience discrimination in society. When people identify with different privileged and marginalized groups, theorists call that intersectionality. Some people cannot separate their identities when speaking about disability.[130] This is salient to understand in communicating with people who have disabilities. I follow Rajkumar's best practices when interacting with the families on my caseload.

127 Shurti Rajkumar, "How to Talk about Disability Sensitively and Avoid Ableist Tropes," *National Public Radio*, August 8, 2022, accessed August 26, 2022, https://www.npr. org/2022/08/08/1115682836/how-to-talk-about-disability-sensitively-and-avoid-ableist-tropes.
128 Ibid.
129 Ibid.
130 Ibid.

My caseload includes families that are culturally and/or linguistically diverse. Imagine seeing or hearing someone who looks and talks like you do. It adds a warm fuzzy feeling through someone's heart. The moment the families who speak Spanish heard me say "Hola, soy Karina," their faces lit up bright like the sun. The families that are African American saw that I was someone of color, they immediately started to speak more comfortably. They no longer felt like they were standing in a crooked room all by themselves.[131]

The way one speaks to people with disabilities makes a significant impact on how the interaction or conversation goes. Eye level, body language, and gestures go a long way. Speaking to someone at their level while making eye contact makes them feel heard. Being interactive with body language makes them feel accepted. Adding gestures so they can understand more than just words, makes them feel seen. One person who did this for me while I was going through college is Dr. LaVonne Neal. She spoke to my peers and I at eye level and her body language made me feel like I was heard. I responded well to her mentorship because I felt like she was hearing and understanding who I was as a person. She knew how to help me succeed. "I truly don't know how I will ever thank Dr. Neal enough for all the encouragement she has provided. The mentorship sessions enhance my focus and help me stay on the right path, and I will forever be grateful."[132]

Dr. Gay stated that the failure to recognize these basic facts all but assures negative results of efforts to improve the education and mental health of students of color.[133] All in all, a failure to recognize that speaking to people with disabilities in a way they will understand results in diminished or zero communication. Dr. Gay emphasizes how meaningful communication enhances the humanity of others. "Communication is the quintessential way to which humans make

131 LaVonne I. Neal, Sarah Militz-Frielink, Alicia L. Moore, Karina Avila, Maria Colompos, Shanell Walter, *Borders, Bras, and Battles: A Practical Guide to Mentor Undergraduate Women to Achieve Career Success* (Loyola University Maryland: Apprentice House, 2016), 1.
132 Ibid, 42.
133 Geneva Gay, "Culturally Responsive Teaching in Special Education for Ethnically Diverse Students: Setting the Stage."

meaningful connections with one another, whether as caring, sharing, loving, teaching, or learning."[134]

Today when I visit my clients of color, I still see their faces and their families faces light up. They are overjoyed to have someone who will understand them simply by speaking to them and understanding their background. These families feel comfortable calling me and talking to me about their needs, and I am more than happy to interact with them. We all come from different ways of life, and having a disability does not make anyone different, it makes them unique.

---

134 Gay Geneva, *Culturally Responsive Teaching: Theory, Research, and Practice* (New York, Teachers College Press, 2018), 93.

# CHAPTER 5

# Personal Accounts of the Integration of Culturally Responsive Teaching into Teaching Methods

*By Greg Wiggan, Annette Teasdell, Tierra Parsons*

In this chapter we discuss and explain the contributions of Dr. Geneva Gay in regards to teacher pedagogy and teaching methods. The chapter is organized into three parts. In Part I, we explain our educational journeys, our introduction to Gay and other Black educators, as well as how Gay has influenced the field of education. In Part II, we provide insights on Gay's culturally responsive teaching framework. In Part III we further reflect on Gay's influence on our teaching practices and methods.

### Part I: Educational Journey in Culturally Responsive Teaching

Hailing from Jamaica, an island in the Caribbean, I (Greg Wiggan) was always taught the importance and value of an education. In 1962 Jamaica gained its independence from British colonial rule. This marked a long history of struggle against slavery and colonial oppression. As a young "independent" country, only a small group of people received an education, and in many cases this was what Dr. Carter G. Woodson coined as miseducation, meaning indoctrination and the influence of European thinking under the guise of education.

Therefore, true education is needed. In the context of slavery, colonialism, and systems of oppression, schools were not a priority of the oppressors, as they were purposeful in keeping the oppressed illiterate and in a state of confusion regarding their true identity, as well as their true heritage and culture. Perhaps, one thing all oppressed groups have in common, is that they have all generally been denied access to a quality education, as this was viewed as being a dangerous endeavor by their oppressor. Illiterate and unexposed, perhaps were the desires of the oppressor because this would create the conditions that would make colonialism last even longer than physical slavery. The chain on the mind would be the apex of group domination.

Since Europeans enslaved and/or colonized more than 80% of the world, education was viewed as a key to true freedom and social progress, as well as to mitigate against Eurocentrism and general whitewashing of history and Black and Brown people's culture.[135] Steve Biko, a powerful social thinker and activist explains that: "the most powerful weapon in the hands of the oppressor, is the mind of the oppressed."[136] As such, education is viewed seriously as a tool of liberation, as well as to disrupt cultural hegemony.

In school, the two educators who have impacted me the most are Mrs. Lyons (Jamaica) and Dr. Asa G. Hilliard (United States). With the support of my parents, my grandmother enrolled all of her grandchildren in the school of Mrs. Lyons, my first teacher, who was a respected educator in Savannah-la-mar, Westmoreland, Jamaica. Mrs. Lyons was very kind and loving, and she was also firm and held high standards and expectations.

Almost twenty years after being a student of Mrs. Lyons, I was placed in the care of another great educator, my last teacher and mentor, Dr. Asa G. Hilliard, for whom the American Educational Research Association *Research Course on African Americans and Education* is named (along with Barbara Sizemore, another powerful educator).

---

135 Wiggan, "In Search of a Canon: European History and the Imperialist State."
136 Biko, "I Like What"

This time it was in a different country (U.S.) and space, but somehow the sensibilities surrounding the notions of cultural praxis and pedagogy as art of teaching and tool of cultural engagement in the classroom were key. As a doctoral student, I was introduced to the work of Dr. Geneva Gay by Dr. Asa G. Hilliard, who was himself a master teacher.

In ninth grade, I (Annette Teasdell) was privileged to study with another perhaps lesser-known master teacher who changed my life. Mrs. Vera Bodison, a high school English teacher at the time, introduced me to Toni Morrison's *The Bluest Eye*. For a young, Black girl like me living in the South Carolina Lowcountry, books that included images reflecting my cultural background and upbringing were rare. This award-winning novel opened my eyes to the experiences of Black women and girls, which broadened my understanding of the world around me. Though I did not recognize it then, I blossomed and learned so much from Mrs. Bodison's teaching practices which incorporated Langston Hughes' "Mother to Son" and "Harlem", while simultaneously planting a seed in me and opening my eyes to how education can be a pathway to freedom.

The Lowcountry was known for its restrictions on educational freedom. *The Stono Rebellion* of 1739 was a major revolt involving South Carolina's Black majority who intended to take over the port of Charleston to gain passage to freedom in St. Augustine where the Spanish promised liberation.[137] Even though the revolt was not successful, it put fear in the hearts of Whites such that the state legislature instituted the Slave Codes of 1740 which forbade travel without written permission, group gatherings without the presence of Whites, forbade teaching enslaved Africans to read and write, and forbade the use of the talking drum. As James Anderson explains in *The Education of Blacks in the South*, this was not the end of restrictions on educational access. [138] The *1954 Brown v. Board of Education* decision, which

---

137 Wood, "Negroes In Colonial"
138 Anderson, "The Education"

included the original case of an eight-year-old Black girl named Linda Carol Brown. In spite of the Supreme Court ruling, gaining access to high-quality education was a challenge for Blacks.

With these examples of educators who changed the world and with the encouragement of Mrs. Bodison, I saw the power of teaching as a means to transform lives. Books in Mrs. Bodison's classroom reflected the students she taught and were my earliest identification with culturally responsive teaching. As Toni Morrison notes: "Books are a form of political action. Books are knowledge. Books are reflection. Books change your mind."

From Jamaica to the U.S., these experiences and educational practices speak to Geneva Gay and culturally responsive education. Gay's book, *Culturally Responsive Teaching* has impacted multicultural education (ME) in a revolutionary way. Based on WorldCat data, Gay's *Culturally Responsive Teaching* is held in over 3,100 libraries around the world. As such, we honor her, as she stands with other civil rights pioneers in education in helping to change schools and society in a positive way. Gay is an internationally renowned scholar whose work has been cited by thousands of researchers. According to ProQuest, as of 2020 over 106,000 doctoral dissertations cite her work.[139] This is an outstanding contribution which speaks to a long legacy and struggle for freedom and inclusion.

## Civil Rights Leaders and Pioneers in Education

Owing to this legacy, we do not intend to set up false binaries nor choose between our heroes and sheroes (an intent of the oppressor), for they have all contributed to the advancement of education. We will not choose between Malcolm X and Dr. Martin Luther King or Ida B. Wells Barnett and Sojourner Truth, for a house divided against itself will not stand. As such, we honor all those who have contributed to the struggle of advancing minority and Black issues in education and beyond. As noted, I (Greg Wiggan) was first introduced to the

139 ProQuest: https://www.proquest.com/

seminal work of Geneva Gay more than two decades ago by my last teacher, Dr. Asa G. Hilliard. Below we pay homage to some of the luminaries and civil rights leaders and pioneers in education as a context for our discussion on Geneva Gay. Again, we do not wish to reify any false binaries, but to honor those who have helped to open the door to educational freedom.

Asa G. Hilliard was a prominent "historian, psychologist and teacher", and he leaves a legacy that emphasizes education as one of the cornerstones in the African American quest for freedom and self-discovery.[140] Hilliard's "theoretical and conceptual contributions led to the formation of an African-centered pedagogy that serves as means for African descended people to affirm and assert their agency." [141] The gravity of Hilliards' legacy underscores the work that must be done to continue exploring the "methods and the content of the socialization processes that we ought to have in place to create wholeness within African American culture." [142]

Similarly, Gloria Ladson-Billings has "championed the production of scholarly work on building strategies in teaching African-American children." [143] [144] Ladson-Billings is "best known for coining the term *culturally relevant pedagogy*"-affirming the value of emphasizing student learning and academic achievement over classroom and behavior management practices. [145] [146] [147] Ladson-Billings "credits her tenacity and the focused direction in her life to her parents and grandparents who nurtured her social and educational capabilities."[148]

Like Gay and Ladson-Billings, James A. Banks has also made a great contribution. Known as the "father of multicultural education," Banks has been "a leader in higher education whose pioneering research

140 Jamison, "Asa Hilliard"
141 Jamison, "Asa Hilliard," 3.
142 African American Literature Book Club, "Asa G. Hilliard".
143 National Academy of Education, "Gloria"
144 deSilva et al., "Igniting Student Learning," 14
145 Ladson-Billings, "Toward a Theory,".
146 Ladson-Billings, "Culturally Relevant"
147 Teachers College-Columbia, "The Suburban"
148 deSilva et al., "Igniting Student Learning," 14

in multicultural education (ME) has yielded profound insights into a vital realm of teaching and learning." [149] [150] [151] As a "leader in the fields of social studies education and multicultural education," Banks' professional and scholarly efforts, to include his numerous publications, editorial contributions and professional memberships, have aided in the improvement of "race and ethnic relations within schools, colleges, and universities throughout the United States and the world." [152] Gay has also contributed greatly to ME, and teacher pedagogy, which we will discuss later in the chapter.

Similarly, Carl A. Grant, a key pioneer in ME, has a distinguished career spanning more than three decades of "researching, teaching, thinking and writing about some of the key enduring issues in multicultural education." [153] [154] In addition to ME, Grant's research interests include "social justice, globalization, and intersectionality" as they are prevalent throughout society today. [155] Grant's work has inspired many educational professionals "to improve students' achievement, enrich their knowledge and skill set in multicultural social justice, culturally responsive curriculum development, and teaching."[156]

Jacqueline Jordan Irvine is also a pioneer and specializes in multicultural and urban teacher education, distinctly in the education of African American students. [157] [158] Like Gay, Irvine has numerous publications in the field of education and has also received many distinguished career awards for her exemplary contributions in the field of ME and her social justice advocacy efforts in educational research. [159]

Similarly, Joyce E. King is widely respected in the fields of urban education and the sociology of education. King's contribution to ME

149 Kansas State University, "Father of Multiculturalism".
150 National Academy of Education, "James Banks".
151 UW College of Education, "James A. Banks".
152 UW College of Education, "James A. Banks".
153 Routledge, "Multiculturalism," para. 2
154 Sage Publishing, "Carl A. Grant".
155 Grant, "Cultivating Flourishing," 910
156 Sage Publishing, "Carl A. Grant".
157 Learning for Justice, "Jacqueline"
158 National Academy of Education, "Jacqueline"
159 National Academy of Education, "Jacqueline".

speaks to the discourse on dysconscious racism. King "previously held senior academic affairs positions as Provost at Spelman College, Associate Provost at Medgar Evers College, CUNY and Associate Vice Chancellor for Academic Affairs and Diversity Programs at the University of New Orleans" [160] King has also served as the Benjamin E. Mays Endowed Chair for Urban Teaching, Learning and Leadership and Professor of Educational Policy Studies in the College of Education & Human Development at Georgia State University." [161] King has been "recognized for her work around racial equity and justice in American education" and Heritage Knowledge as associated with her many publications, editorial contributions as well as her training and consulting professional commitments. [162] [163] [164]

Also, Lisa Delpit, "education researcher, author, visionary scholar and reformer, has worked ardently to promote anti-oppressive teaching practices and reforms to language and literary education." [165] Delpit has received numerous accolades and has held many distinguished appointments to include being named a MacArthur Fellow, the Benjamin E. Mays Chair of Urban Educational Leadership at Georgia State University and executive director/eminent scholar for the Center for Urban Education & Innovation. Delpit has also been a "consultant for public school systems, colleges, and community groups across the country," advancing the advocacy agenda for educational access for students of color. [166] [167] We honor all of these giants, as collectively they have advanced the educational and social progress of Black children around the globe.

## Geneva Gay and the Art of Culturally Responsive Teaching

In our assessment, what these pioneers have in common with

160 King, "Dr. Joyce E. King," para. 4.
161 King, "Dr. Joyce E. King," para. 4.
162 Georgia State University, "Joyce E. King".
163 King, "Dr. Joyce E. King,".
164 Stanford Graduate School of Education, "Joyce E. King," para. 1.
165 Harvard Graduate School of Education, "A Visionary".
166 Harvard Graduate School of Education, "A Visionary".
167 MacArthur Foundation, "Lisa Delpit".

Geneva Gay is a commitment to high quality education for Black children. Geneva Gay, Emerita Professor of Education at the University of Washington-Seattle, is a nationally and internationally renowned leader, expert and prominent figure in the field of education, whose global influence on culturally relevant and culturally responsive teaching has impacted the learning and academic success of a myriad of students as well as contributed to the pedagogical efficiency of many teachers from diverse backgrounds. [168] [169] [170] Always kind and gracious, I (Greg Wiggan) can remember one of my encounters with Geneva Gay at an Association for the Study of African American Life and History (ASALH) Conference in Cincinnati, Ohio [2017]. We met in the lobby of the hotel and I humbly offered to take her bags for her. Kind and gracious, we talked delightfully. Later that evening, I watched Gay teach with mastery a room full of public school teachers and students in a large auditorium. I (Greg Wiggan) thought, "wow, Geneva Gay is always so impressive and humble, and approachable!" Gay is distinctly recognized for her scholarship in ME in the areas of staff development, curriculum design, classroom instruction, and the nature of culture and learning. [171] [172] [173]

Born and raised in northeast Georgia, Gay attended "all Black elementary, middle school and high schools" during a time when "part of her town was still very much segregated." [174] After completing high school, Gay moved to Akron, Ohio to attend The University of Akron where she received her bachelor's degree in comprehensive social studies and later her master's degree in contemporary United States history and the Middle East. [175] [176] Following graduate school, Gay devoted her time to establishing her career as a high school social

168 Mensah, "Culturally Relevant".
169 UW College of Education, "Geneva Gay".
170 UW College of Education,"Faculty".
171 Mensah, "Culturally Relevant".
172 Teachers College Press, ""Geneva Gay".
173 UW College of Education, "Geneva Gay"
174 UW College of Education, "Faculty".
175 Atwater, "Dr. Geneva Gay".
176 UW College of Education, "Faculty"

studies teacher in an Akron, Ohio urban school system where she sparked her commitment to "embedding multicultural education and cultural diversity into programs and curricula." [177] [178] Gay's decision to pursue her doctorate degree in Education from The University of Texas at Austin was driven by her pursuit of self-discovery and her motivation to find deeper meaning into the lived experiences of her "Black students". [179] [180]

In addition to her contributions to secondary education, Gay's professional experiences extend to include her work as a university professor, her authorship with national education publishers, her membership with multiple editorial and review boards and her expertise as a consultant for schools, professional organizations, and teacher education programs across the U.S. and internationally on the topic of culturally responsive pedagogy. [181] [182] [183] Gay has also notably published "more than 140 articles, book chapters, monographs, and book reviews in the area of multicultural education." [184]

Gay is an internationally renowned scholar whose work has been cited by thousands of scholars. According to ProQuest, as of 2020 over 106,000 doctoral dissertations cite her work. Based on WorldCat data, Gay's *Cultural Responsive Teaching* is held in over 3,100 libraries around the world. [185] Gay has been the recipient of several distinguished awards to include the 1990 Distinguished Scholar Award, presented by the Committee on the Role and Status of Minorities in Educational Research and Development of the American Educational Research Association; the inaugural 1994 Multicultural Educator Award, presented by the National Association of Multicultural Education; the 2004 W. E. B. Du Bois Distinguished Lecturer Award presented by

177 Atwater, "Dr. Geneva Gay".
178 UW Washington, "Faculty".
179 Atwater, "Dr. Geneva Gay, 161.
180 Gay, "Faculty".
181 Atwater, "Dr. Geneva Gay".
182 Learning for Justice, "Geneva Gay".
183 Teachers College Press, ""Geneva Gay".
184 Atwater, "Dr. Geneva Gay," 162.
185 WorldCat, https://www.worldcat.org/

the Special Interest Group on Research Focus on Black Education of the American Educational Research Association and the 2006 Mary Anne Raywid Award for Distinguished Scholarship in the Field of Education presented by the Society of Professors of Education. [186] [187] [188] She is also recipient of the ASALH Life Time Achievement Award. Still, Gay remains committed to the integrity, credibility, purpose of ME through her continued dedication to promoting the "rights, benefits, and opportunities of students of color." [189]

Our purpose in Part I has been to enlighten others on our journeys and how Geneva Gay and others have influenced the field of education. In Part II, we provide insights on Gay's culturally responsive teaching theory. In Part III, we further reflect on Gay's influence on our teaching, and we provide implications for teacher pedagogy.

## Part II: Culturally Responsive Teaching Methods and Practices

For decades, educational leaders and pioneers we mentioned earlier in this chapter have been invested in the prioritization of culturally informed pedagogy and practice in education. According to Gay, "culture is at the heart of all we do in the name of education, whether that is curriculum, instruction, administration or performance." [190] Culture also "encompasses many things, some of which are important for teachers to know than others because they have implications for teaching and learning." [191] In order to appropriately address the culturally diverse implications for teaching and learning, "advocates speak convincingly about the need to prepare teachers to function more effectively with ethnically, racially, culturally and socially diverse students and issues."[192] One critical, intersectional issue that teachers and administrators most often navigate that is unique to students of

---

186 Atwater, "Dr. Geneva Gay,".
187 Teachers College Press, ""Geneva Gay".
188 UW College of Education, "Geneva Gay".
189 Atwater, "Dr. Geneva Gay," 162.
190 Gay, "Culturally Responsive Teaching," 49.
191 Gay, "Culturally Responsive Teaching," 107.
192 Gay, "Politics of Multicutural Teacher, " 227.

color is related to academic underachievement ,[193] [194] [195] [196] [197] [198] [199] [200] a motivating factor that inspired the "beginning" of culturally responsive teaching.[201]

Culturally responsive teaching, as forwarded by Geneva Gay, "provides suggestions to reversing the underachievement of students of color.[202] According to Gay, there are many "alternative beliefs that can explain the underachievement of students of color and poverty that offer more constructive directions for instructional change" to include:

> *Cultural incompatibilities between schools and homes of ethnically and racially diverse students; stress and anxiety associated with continually crossing cultural boundaries between home and school; the existential gap between students and teachers due to such factors as race, class, gender, age, education, ethnicity, and residence; the absence of ethnic and cultural diversity in school programs, practices and personnel; ethnically diverse students' perceptions of schools as hostile, unfriendly, and uncaring; and significant variability in students' access to and mastery of the social capital of schooling.*[203]

Given that "culture strongly influences the attitudes, values and behaviors that students and teachers bring to the instructional process, it has to likewise be a major determinant of how the problems of underachievement are solved."[204] Cheesman and Pry posit that "attempts to close achievement gaps have resulted in school reform

193 Bruce et al., "Closing the Gap".
194 Gay, "Culturally Responsive Teaching".
195 Gay, "Preparing for Culturally Responsive".
196 Gay, "The What, Why and How".
197 Howard and Reynolds, "Examining Parent".
198 Jackson, "Unlocking the Potential".
199 Smith, "School Factors that Contribute".
200 Swartz, "Helping Underachieving Boys".
201 Gay, "Culturally Responsive Teaching; Ideas".
202 Gay, "Culturally Responsive Teaching," 34
203 Gay, "Teaching To and Through," 55.
204 Gay, "Preparing for Culturally Responsive," 114.

efforts to include culturally responsive teaching." [205] Culturally responsive teaching is defined as "a teacher's ability to use the characteristics, existing and former experiences, frames of reference, perspectives and performance styles of ethnically diverse students to increase the interest, meaning, relevance, ease and effectiveness of learning experiences" [206] [207] [208] and is "best understood as a response to traditional curricular and instructional methods that have often been ineffective for students of color, immigrant children, and students from lower socioeconomic families." [209]

Culturally responsive teaching is based on five essential elements: "(1) developing a knowledge base about cultural diversity, (2) including ethnic and cultural diversity content in the curriculum, (3) demonstrating caring and building learning communities, (4) communicating with ethnically diverse students, and (5) responding to ethnic diversity in the delivery of instruction." [210] These elements were designed to help schools, through pedagogy and practice, fully advance the purpose of culturally responsive teaching in schools; however, Gay [211] states that, "teachers must be adequately prepared and understand existing obstacles to culturally responsive teaching." The elements are illustrated below:

205 Cheesman and Pray, "A Critical Review," 84.
206 Gay, "Preparing for Culturally Responsive".
207 Gay, "Culturally Responsive Teaching".
208 Gay, "Teaching To and Through".
209 Vavrus, "Culturally Responsive Teaching," 49.
210 Gay, "Preparing for Culturally Responsive," 106.
211 Gay, "Preparing for Culturally Responsive," 106-108.

# 5 Elements: Culturally Responsive Teaching
(Gay, 2000, p. 106)

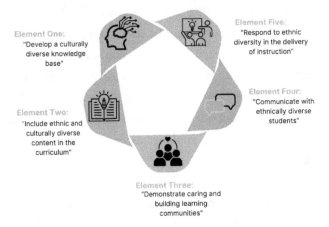

Element One:
"Develop a culturally
diverse knowledge
base"

Element Five:
"Respond to ethnic
diversity in the delivery
of instruction"

Element Two:
"Include ethnic and
culturally diverse
content in the
curriculum"

Element Four:
"Communicate with
ethnically diverse
students"

Element Three:
"Demonstrate caring and
building learning
communities"

Based on these elements, Gay suggests ways to prepare teachers to include "revising curriculum and instructional materials for better representations of cultural diversity," "creating culturally conducive classroom climates for ethnically diverse students," "practicing and promoting cross-cultural communication between the teacher and the students" and "delivering culturally inclusive instruction." [212] According to Gay,[213] "one of the most important premises of culturally responsive education is teachers' beliefs about ethnic, racial, and cultural diversity determine their instructional behaviors. While culturally responsive teaching is a multi-layered concept with many intersections and cultural underpinning for teachers to navigate, Gay emphasizes the importance of understanding that the inner working will "evolve over time." [214]

Comparable to the "ideas similar to those offered by other proponents of culturally responsive teaching, such as Ladson-Billings, [215] Irvine [216] and Hollins and Oliver, [217] culturally responsive teaching

---

212 Gay, "Preparing for Culturally Responsive," 108-110.
213 Gay, "The What the Why," 126.
214 Gay, "Teaching To and Through," 57.
215 Ladson-Billings, "Toward a Theory".
216 Irvine, "Educating Teachers for Diversity".
217 Hollins and Oliver, "Pathways to Success".

makes clear the significance of "highlighting the positive learning possibilities of marginalized students and their heritage groups instead of belaboring their problems and pathologies."[218] Moreover, Gay affirms that, "positive attitudes about ethnic, racial and gender differences generate positive instructional expectations and actions toward diverse students, which, in turn, have positive effects on students' learning efforts and outcomes."[219] Gay further asserts that, "students, especially underachieving ones, need opportunities to gain knowledge and learn skills that they can apply in life and how to meet high standards of academic excellence, rather than wasting time on fanciful notions about cultural diversity."[220] The lens through which to view the possibilities of life changing educational and social opportunities for students is framed by Gay's idea that:

> *Culturally responsive teaching requires replacing pathological and deficient perceptions of students and communities of color with more positive ones. While the problems and challenges these populations face in society and schools must be addressed they should not be the only emphasis. Educational innovations motivated by and framed only in negativism do not generate constructive and sustainable achievement transformations for ethnically and culturally diverse students.[221]*

All students, to include students of color, should have "access to equitable opportunities to learn and meet high standards."[222] These particular opportunities and academic aims are made possible through the active involvement of teachers from diverse backgrounds who consider the students to be benefactors of their efforts.[223]

Although, "research, theory, and practice attest to the potential effectiveness of culturally responsive teaching suggestions (i.e. teacher

218 Gay, "Teaching To and Through," 50-51
219 Gay, "Teaching To and Through," 56
220 Gay, "Culturally Responsive Teaching," 74.
221 Gay, "Teaching To and Through," 54.
222 Banks et al., "Diversity Within Unity," 2.
223 Gay, "Culturally Responsive Teaching," 72.

preparation, cross-cultural communication), culturally responsive teaching alone cannot solve all the problems of improving the education of marginalized students of color."[224] Gay underscores the value of continuity among different societal groups on the quest to promoting and advancing equity and excellence in education by asserting that, "culturally responsiveness is a rallying cry for many different service professions in pursuit of more equity and effectiveness in the work they do for and with diverse groups."[225] It is important for all educational stakeholders to understand that responding to this "rally cry" will involve, "insisting that the disempowerment of students of color stop now and set into motion change strategies to ensure that it does."[226]

While research has shown that action-based efforts to promote culturally responsive teaching in education are beneficial, [227] [228] [229] [230] Gay states that:

> *Teachers need to know that there is a lot of opposition to culturally responsive teaching. It has different causes and takes varied forms. These can range from benign ambiguities and uncertainties about engaging in cultural diversity, to explicit rejection of its reality and value in education… Part of the challenge to culturally responsive teaching is confronting resistance without simultaneously diverting attention and effort away from promoting cultural diversity.[231]*

Even though resistance to culturally responsive teaching may exist, to include the "demands it imposes for envisioning ways to achieve better learning, culturally responsive teaching is empowering

---

224 Gay, "Culturally Responsive Teaching," 34.
225 Gay, "The What, Why and How," 124.
226 Gay, "Culturally Responsive Teaching," 34.
227 Gay, "Culturally Responsive Teaching".
228 Gay, "Preparing for Culturally Responsive".
229 Gay, "The What, The Why and How".
230 Gay, "Culturally Responsive Teaching: Ideas".
231 Gay, Teaching To and Through," 56.

and benefits everyone!"[232] [233] This culturally responsive worldview is, "a means for unleashing the higher learning potentials of ethnically diverse students by simultaneously cultivating their academic and psychosocial abilities."[234] As we begin to shape our work in education with students of color, Gay reminds us that:

> Culture and difference are an unconditional part of
> their human heritage. As the life cycle unfolds they may,
> for various reasons, modify or embellish their social and
> human inheritances but they cannot choose to be or not
> to be cultural and different. Therefore it is futile for
> educators to claim that they can attend to the needs of
> students (for academic learning and otherwise) without
> engaging their cultural socialization, and expect students
> to divorce themselves from their heritages easily and at
> will.[235]

Culture has everything to do with promoting and ensuring equity and access in education, it is just up to educators and those invested in the future of education to adopt this idea as their educational truth. Through the transformative and liberating pathways of culturally responsive teaching, education will become a place where all students of color are able to boldly lead, thrive and reach their full potential.[236]

## Other Culturally Responsive Teaching Practices

Addressing cultural, social and systemic issues in education through the influence of Culturally responsive teaching has led to the emergence of other culturally responsive teaching practices in academia such as: culturally appropriate instruction,[237] culturally congruent pedagogy,[238] and cultural compatibility.[239]

232 Gay, 'Culturally Responsive Teaching," 96.
233 Gay, "The What, The Why and How," 136.
234 Gay, "Culturally Responsive Teaching," 72.
235 Gay, "Teaching To and Through," 61.
236 Gay, "Culturally Responsive Teaching," 96-102.
237 Au and Jordan, "Teaching Reading to Hawaiian".
238 Mohatt and Erickson, "Cultural Differences in Teaching".
239 Jordan, "Translating Culture."

## Culturally Appropriate Instruction

As one of the hallmarks of education, classroom instruction has been an important catalyst for driving student comprehension and achievement. Ensuring the cultural responsiveness of instruction can better help students of color with different educational needs. According to Singh, a culturally appropriate education melds instruction to better fit the expectations and cultural patterns of the group being served" and involves three criteria: 1) comfortability for the students, 2) comfortability for the teachers and 3) the promotion of better acquisition of basic academic skill.[240] To help promote the value of inclusion in education, the group's language, culture, and its worldview are built into the routines, curriculum, and structure of the school. Yazzie posits that:

> *Education researchers and practitioners have long advocated adopting a culturally appropriate curriculum. Such an approach uses materials that link traditional or cultural knowledge originating in Native home life and community to the curriculum of the school. Deeply embedded cultural values drive curriculum development and implementation and help determine which subject matter and skills will receive the most classroom attention.[241]*

In addition to adopting a culturally appropriate curriculum, another important aspect of culturally appropriate instruction is that it helps to, "bridge the gap between the school and the world of the student, is consistent with the values of the students' own culture aimed at assuring academic learning, and encourages teachers to adapt their instruction to meet the learning needs of all students." [242]

## Culturally Congruent Pedagogy

Through their research and pedagogical experiences in education,

240 Singh, "Culturally Appropriate," 14.
241 Yazzie, "Culturally Appropriate Curriculum," 2.
242 Callins, "Culturally Responsive Literacy," 63.

Mohatt and Erickson found culture to be an important factor among students of color related to their school experience, hence the development of the term culturally congruent pedagogy (CCP). [243] CCP "represents a promising approach to socially just teaching" in schools and is defined as "the harmony or alignment among the participation structures, language use, and learning styles experienced in the home and at school." [244] According to Au and Kawakami:

> *Culturally congruence in instruction does not mean an attempt to replicate a home or community environment in the classroom. Research on cultural congruence recognizes that the home and school are different settings with different functions in students' lives. Culturally congruent educational practices incorporate features of the student' home culture but do not result in activities and environments identical to those of the home.* [245]

Research has shown that when introducing and implementing culturally congruent pedagogy in schools with learners from culturally diverse backgrounds, it is important for teachers to receive the training needed to gain the knowledge, develop the best approach and cultivate the creativity needed to maximize the students' educational experiences.[246]

## Cultural Compatibility

Research has shown that "culture influences expectations about classroom goals and influences the social environment of classrooms in many ways."[247] The significance of the acknowledgement of culture in the classroom has been emphasized over the years through the concept of cultural compatibility. According to Jordan:

> *cultural compatibility...assumes that to be successful, educational practice must be compatible with the*

243 Mohatt and Erickson, "Cultural Differences in Teaching".
244 Carpenter Ford, "Verbal Ping Pong," 373.
245 Au and Kawakami, "Cultural Congruence," 6.
246 Schonleber, "Culturally Congruent Teaching," 257.
247 Yamauchi, "Individualism, Collectivism and Cultural," 189.

*culture(s) of the children being educated. This means that educational practices must mesh with the children's culture in ways that ensure the generation of academically important behaviors. It does not mean that all school practices need be completely congruent with natal culture practices, in the sense of exactly or even closely matching or agreeing with them. The point of cultural compatibility is that the natal culture is used as a guide...*[248]

Examples of culturally compatible classroom practices include: (1) encouraging and building on natal culture elements, (2) avoid a particular natal culture element in selecting classroom practices (3) ignore classroom manifestations of certain natal culture features that do not contribute to academic work and (4) shape or extend natal culture elements in some way.[249] These culturally compatible classroom practices help to guide our teaching practices. Below we provide personal narratives on how we use culturally responsive teaching in our classrooms.

## Part III: Culturally Responsive Teaching and our Classroom Practices

Regarding Gay's culturally responsive teaching and its five elements, I ( Greg Wiggan) explain my pedagogical practices based on these principles. In light of *Element One: Develop a Culturally Diverse Knowledge Base*, in the classroom I seek to raise students' awareness concerning the richness of their own culture as well as others. In this sense, I try to emphasize that all cultures have *great* value, as they speak directly to the human experience, as well as to all social groups. Towards this end, it is important to deconstruct and disrupt misconceptions regarding Eurocentrism and general cultural and/or racial superiority claims. As such, I emphasize an appreciation for

248 Jordan, "Translating Culture," 110.
249 Jordan, "Translating Culture," 113-114.

the contributions of all cultures, and that they should be viewed as assets rather than deficits. Next, in light of Gay's *Element Two: Include Ethnic and Culturally Diverse Content in the Curriculum,* in the classroom I like to draw awareness to the preponderance of evidence which suggests that Africa is the birthplace of humanity, and that written language and some of the oldest books in the world are found in the continent. For example, *Teaching of PtahHotep, Oldest Book in the World; Egyptian Book of the Coming Forth by Day and Night,* also mistakenly called *The Book of the Dead* by Europeans; *Papyrus of Ani,* among others. Disrupting and breaking down misconceptions help students' growth and development. Students are often reflective as they realize that all humans share 99.9% of the same **deoxyribonucleic acid (DNA)**, this can help mitigate racist educational and societal discourse, and even *curriculum violence,* deliberate manipulation of academic programming which compromises the intellectual or psychological well-being of learners.[250] I emphasize that the goal is exposure and not to impose on anyone. Students are encouraged to do their own research. As such, I actively seek and include curriculum materials that reflect a variety of cultures and artifacts as such: Olmec, *The Teachings of PtahHotep,* Imhotep, The Rhind Manuscript (Ahmes Manuscript), etc. These are often on display for reflection and examination. I emphasize students' natural genius and I try to create opportunities for self-discovery and transformation.

In light of Gay's *Element Three: Demonstrate Caring and Building Learning Communities,* an effective teacher seeks to create a safe space for learners. It is not always comfortable to discuss sensitive topics such as intersections of race, class, gender, sexuality, immigrant status, religion, spirituality, etc. and their implications for education. However, this is work that must be done to help advance an inclusive society. This is challenging work. Nevertheless, I try to nurture the environment of a Think-Tank, rather than a classroom to create a shared space regarding a community of learners. In this light, students

---

250 Ighodaro & Wiggan, "Curriculum Violence"

are joint facilitators of knowledge and we try to unpack challenging school and societal issues (e.g. school force out, teacher shortage, curriculum violence, school-to-prison pipeline, school reform), and find solutions to them. Also, in the spirit of growth and development, I also emphasize personal care and wellness, eating healthy, exercising, and mindful meditation practices (see *The Healing Power of Education* by Watson Vandiver and Wiggan).

In regards to Gay's *Element Four: Communication with Ethnically Diverse Students,* I try to highlight the cultures and ethnicities we have in the classroom as assets. In this sense, culture is viewed as a basis of a person's ethnic identity. Since some cultures have been particularly marginalized and omitted from educational discourse, I attempt to re-center them. As noted earlier in this chapter, in the case of colonized and oppressed groups, we must be purposeful in bringing their voices and artifacts into the classroom. To achieve this goal, in the classroom we honor and respect linguistic differences. I treat language as power, and as such, it must be used in a positive and uplifting way. And finally, regarding Gay's *Fifth Element: Respond to Ethnic Diversity in the Delivery of Instruction,* in the classroom I try to use examples in teaching that include representation of ethnically diverse students. This also means using readings and artifacts that speak directly to diversity and inclusion. For example, books such as: *Gifted, Little Paul Laurence: The Boy Genius, Little John goes to College,* and others can provide useful multicultural narratives. Additionally, I allow students to report based on culturally responsive projects they create that reflect their ethnic diversity.

For me (Annette Teasdell), Geneva Gay's contribution to multicultural education is analogous to a tree that has born many fruits but still continues to rest on a strong foundation for teaching excellence yielding improved student outcomes in U.S. public schools. An examination of Gay's tenets reveals that her contributions have a ripple effect that has emboldened my (Annette Teasdell) practice and is certain to enhance teacher pedagogy for years to come. I expose students to the richness of their own culture by incorporating into the curriculum thematic content that can dually increase their appreciation for the contributions of cultures.

It is not sufficient to just talk about the contributions of Black culture in the curriculum but to start from the beginning. Therefore, curriculum reform should address the way missing narratives promote a "single story" which begins at some point other than the beginning and does not provide an accurate account of the multiple perspectives that inform human history.[251] Since Africa is the origin of the human family tree and civilization, teaching a curriculum that reflects this has informed my practice. A curriculum that reflects multiple perspectives creates opportunities for personal growth.

What I (Annette Teasdell) have learned in my practice is that relationship building and creating spaces where everyone contributes is essential. When students feel connected to a learning community that values their unique contributions, they are more engaged. My teaching philosophy is based on the premise that the teacher is a facilitator and an active participant in the learning process. Given students' diverse backgrounds, their unique experiences inform and expand the educational environment. The teaching model centers the learning so that teachers and students are joint facilitators of knowledge. Culturally responsive teaching makes learning come alive for students such that education is a lifelong journey.

In summation, we thank Dr. Geneva Gay for her many contributions and for her enduring legacy as a multicultural and culturally responsive educator. Through her work, she has influenced the teaching practices of thousands of educators and countless students. We thank you for your service, and for your grace and humility, as a noble servant. Thank you!

---

251 Adichie, "The Danger"

# Part III

The Impact of Culturally Responsive
Teaching on Policy

# CHAPTER 6

# Policy and Governance Structures: The Infusion of Culturally Responsive Teaching

*By: Regina A. Lewis, Shanell Walter, and Erika Lourenco de Freitas*

## Introduction

Regina Lewis, a professor and entrepreneur; Captain Shanell Walter, a U.S. Army human resources officer; and Erika Lourenco de Freitas, an Assistant Dean; three distinctively different professionals converged their voices together to infuse the tenants of Geneva Gay's work as a guide for schools and organizations to incorporate culturally responsive policy into their everyday operations. In each of their organizations, they have identified challenges and incorporated organizational change by effectively responding to ethnic diversity in the system of their respective organizations.

One may argue that embracing a culturally responsive organization is a systemic problem. To address systemic problems takes systemic solutions. Systems are made up of many interrelated connections and interactions of policies, procedures, and practices. The question is how do we respond to culture within these objectives? Being that policy sets parameters for decision making within an organization, examining policy sets the standard for ensuring culturally responsive interactions are infused at every level of the organization.

## Defining Culturally Responsive Policy

Based on Gay's work, culturally responsive policy uses "cultural characteristics, experiences, and perspectives of ethnically diverse [individuals and/or groups] as conduits" for procedures, decision making, communication, and hiring practices within an organization. Converting to culturally responsive policies takes examining and converting current policies into formal, symbolic, and societal [actions of the everyday operations of an organization]." These three types of actions are in line with Gay's "three kinds of curricula." Formal actions are guidelines and standards that focus on the "quantity, accuracy, complexity, placement, purpose, variety, significance, [and authenticity of trainings, procedures, hiring practices, access, opportunities, evaluations, and advancement]." Symbolic action is the "images, symbols, icons, mottoes, awards, celebrations, and other artifacts that are used to create the morals and values which conveys important information about ethnic and cultural diversity [within the organization]."

Keep in mind that it is important that information presented is accurate extensions of the formal actions when incorporating symbolic actions. Lastly, are the "societal [actions]; these are the knowledge, ideas, and impressions about ethnic groups that are portrayed in the media." "Programming, articles, advertisement, and videos whose content reflects and conveys cultural, social, ethnic, and political values, knowledge, and advocacies."

## Culturally Reactive vs Culturally Responsive

Several organizations have expressed interest in or challenges around equity, diversity, and inclusion. Culturally reactive organizations find their attempt of incorporating this work unsuccessful. After training or data has been presented, these organizations struggle with transference of learning resulting in reverting back to learned patterns of behavior and what is referred to as a cultural mindset. A cultural mindset is based on beliefs, behaviors, values, and preferences that make up existing culture and climate of a given organization.

For an organization to become culturally responsive, this requires a cultural mind shift. Not eliminating the values and beliefs of the organization, cultural mind shifting is incorporating multiple perspectives, expanding and adjusting values and beliefs, and examining and reducing the negative impact of bias. Cultural responsiveness involves empathy, humility, and an "explicit knowledge about cultural diversity [which requires] understanding the cultural characteristics and contributions of different ethnic groups."

Geneva Gay states, "Intention without action is insufficient." To move into action is intentional, takes courage, and responding with empathy. According to Kelly Cross, there are four steps in responding with empathy, Step 1 - Connect with existing knowledge, Step 2 – Extend yourself slightly beyond what you know, Step 3 – Be willing to work through cognitive dissonance, and Step 4 – Learn something new.

We discuss the lived experiences of our mindset and the elements within mind shifting. The mindset is first created by all exposure and the experiences within that exposure. Keep in mind, two people within the organization can have the same exposure, but their experience within the exposure can vary and be very different. Experience impacts what is believed and beliefs impact what is valued and what is not. Based on what is valued, thoughts about others are manifested. Cultural mind shifting is first examining and realizing the cultural mindset and allowing new information to become part of the thinking and actions. This means allowing and inviting different perspectives, experiencing difference, and intentionally building empathy. Once these steps are taken, there becomes space for adjusting values and thoughts of others.

**Diagram 1.0**

## Cultural Mindset

Cultural mindsets and cultural mind shifting can apply to individuals as well as organizations.

## Policy Audit Factors

"An equitable [organization] embodies an environment that cultivates practices and content, to enable [employees, customers, and] students to perform at their highest level."[252] Based on the work of María Colompos-Tohtsonie, there are three factors for equitable policy within organizations:

- A quantifiable and direct mission statement, which outlines the priorities of providing equitable access, procedures, treatment, and outcomes for all, regardless of race, ethnicity, gender identity, individual abilities, or socioeconomic status.

- Scaffolds cultural competency of employees and customers through inclusive historical trainings, teachings, and tools of various cultural backgrounds and information resources.

- Collaborates with communities in and outside the organization, officials, and civic organizations to develop support mechanisms and increase knowledge and skills in civic learning, agency, and participation for all within the system.

Grounded in Gay's work there are five essential culturally responsive elements to use within policy.

- Developing a knowledge base about cultural diversity, including ethnic and culturally diverse content.

- Demonstrate care and build learning communities

---

252 N. Bell, "Criteria for an Equitable School–Equity Audit," Mid-Atlantic Equity Consortium, 2016, accessed September 25, 2022, https://maec.org/wp-content/uploads/2016/04/Criteria-for-an-Equitable-School-2020-accessible.pdf

- Communication with ethnically diverse groups

- Respond to ethnic diversity in the delivery of instruction

**Moving to Culturally Responsive Policy**

Moving to culturally responsive policy begins with the examination of multiple cultural data points. Figure 1.0 is a chart of different data points. These data points along with their corresponding conduits for examining policy are grouped together under their perspective action (i.e., formal, symbolic, societal). Findings can be extracted from the aggregated and disaggregated data collected from the action descriptors. See figure 1.0.

The examination of the data will inform strategic planning, goal setting, as well as budgeting. Training managers will be informed of the objectives for trainings and identify specific resources. Human resources will gain knowledge that will impact policy and guide leadership in mandating procedures. Lastly, understanding the impact of current policy that is not culturally responsive will support the need for policy change and readjustment of the organizations budget.

## Figure 1.0    Cultural Action Data Assessment Points

| DATA POINTS | CONDUITS FOR EXAMINING POLICY EFFECTIVELY | ACTION DESCRIPTORS |
| --- | --- | --- |
| **FORMAL** | | |
| Climate Survey | Ethnic perceptions and perspectives of an organization. | Quantity, accuracy, complexity, placement, purpose, variety, significance, and authenticity of trainings, procedures, hiring practices, access, opportunities, evaluations, and advancement. |
| Demographics | Ethnically diverse population within an organization | |
| Assessment | Systematic review of processes, environment, and organizational structure. | |
| **SYMBOLIC** | | |
| Literature | Written work that guides, advises, and represents the Organization's system. | Images, symbols, icons, mottoes, awards, celebrations, and other artifacts that are used to create the morals, values, and conveys important information about ethnic and cultural diversity within the organization. |
| Visual | Seeing a balance of diverse people and groups that include ethnicity represented without hierarchy. | |
| Media/ Marketing | Promoting and marketing that captures, in an authentic way, the ethnic, racial, and age diversity of your people.[253] | |
| Observation | Gaining information within an organization through examining interaction, retention, recruitment, advancement, and interaction of ethnically diverse groups. | |
| **SOCIETAL** | | |

---

253    Warren Epstein (Executive Director of Marketing and Communication) in discussion with author, August, 2022.

| Focus Groups | Culturally informed groups of people assembled in a guided discussion to provide feedback on specific cultural experiences. | Knowledge, ideas, and impressions about ethnic groups that are portrayed in the media. Programing, articles, advertisement, and videos whose content reflects and conveys cultural, social, ethnic, and political values, knowledge, and advocacies. |
|---|---|---|
| Evaluations | Understanding, application, and communication with and about people who ethnically diverse people and groups. | |
| Community | Ethnically diverse groups feelings and beliefs around a sense of belonging, fellowship, common place, interest, and goals within the organization | |
| Leadership | Those who set direction, support an inspiring vision, provide access, and opportunity based on understanding the need, knowledge, and skill within the lived experiences and frames of reference of people who are ethnically diverse and groups. | |

Adapted from the culturally responsive research of Dr. Geneva Gay

This data can inform organizations of systemic challenges and how to approach systemic solutions. Furthermore, this data will inform types of training, tools, and resources needed to create and ensure culturally responsive policy. Adapted by Regina Lewis, Ph.D.

## Impact/Results of Culturally Responsive Policies

When culturally responsive policy is present and enforced, the goals, mission, and vision of an organization can be accomplished. Every part of the system will be impacted, resulting in:

- A sense of belonging

- Fair access and opportunities for advancement

- Fair hiring practices will increase successful hiring of diverse candidates

- Increase in recruitment and retention of candidates who are ethnically diverse

## Professional Approaches to Culturally Responsive Policy

Regina Lewis is the Department Chair of Communication in the Division of Communications, Humanities, and Technical Studies at Pikes Peak State College in Colorado Springs, CO. Her research investigates programs, policies, and practices that maintain cultural excellence, equity, and inclusion in academic and business environments. As department chair, she has diversified faculty using culturally responsive recruitment strategies. It is not enough to advertise for faculty in ethnically diverse locations, schools, and groups, Lewis spends time in these places learning, engaging, and appreciating the cultural nuances and incorporating some of these learned experiences into her everyday work and environment. Building relationships of mutual respect became the conduit for trust, interest, recruitment, advancement, and ultimately retention.

Working at a culturally diverse college where the focus is the success of all students, based on the data, Lewis has found there is a constant disproportionate low success rate for some cultural groups across all disciplines. These statistics are what informed the decision of her research on communalism values and the academic success and retention of African American male students in community college.[254] In her work she examines allocentism and the cultural nine dimensions of Afrocultural expression to understand the various ways African Americans integrate socially and culturally. Having a personal discussion at Howard University in 2009, A. Wade Boykin shared his Black culture ethos with Regina Lewis:

254 Regina Lewis, "Communalism Values and the Academic Success and Retention of the African American Male Students in Community College," PhD, diss. (2010).

1. *Spirituality*: The realization of forces that are powerful.

2. *Harmony*: Emphasizes versatility and wholeness.

3. *Movement*: Interweaving the ideas of rhythm

4. *Verve*: Preferring intense stimulation, variability, and action that are energetic, active, and colorful.

5. *Affect*: Placing a premium on feelings, emphasizing a special sensitivity to emotional cues, and cultivating emotional expression.

6. *Communalism*: Committing to the interdependence of people and to connectedness that esteems social bonds and responsibilities over individual privileges.

7. *Expressive individualism*: Cultivating a distinct personality and a proclivity for spontaneous, and genuine personal expression.

8. *Orality*: Emphasizing oral and aural modes of communication.

9. *Social Time Perspective*: Humankind and the completion of its social events should take precedence over time, rather than become slaves to time.

Evaluating part-time instructors, under Lewis's leadership, there seemed to be a lack of culturally responsive pedagogy in the classrooms, courses, as well as interaction with students. Gay refers to this as "cultural blindness teaching from a middle class, Eurocentric framework that shapes school practices."[255] Students gain more knowledge and are more successful when they have teachers who can relate to their experiences. Within Lewis's department there was an underrepresentation of professors of color. Through her CEID (Cultural Excellence: Ideas

255 Gay Geneva, *Culturally Responsive Teaching: Theory, Research, and Practice*, 21.

and Discussions) program, Lewis worked with the leadership team along with human resources within the college to examine the hiring and lack of culturally represented instructor hiring practices within the policies and procedures. Uncovering the minimum and preferred qualifications within the job announcements perpetuates the belief that "good teachers anywhere are good teachers everywhere."[256]

To address this disparity and to hire culturally responsive teachers, qualifications and interview questions were changed, requiring applicants to address and demonstrate a sufficient amount of knowledge about:

- Cultures of different ethnic groups,

- Treatment of students differently without hierarchy,

- Differentiating learning,

- Acculturation instead of assimilation, and

- Respecting individual differences of all students.

Regina Lewis is also an entrepreneur, owner of ReginaSpeaking, LLC (www.reginaspeaking.com), one of her areas of focus is intercultural communication. As a trainer, facilitator, and executive coach, her philosophy in doing this work is based on what she refers to as her BRIC Approach-Building Rich and Inclusive Cultures. A brick is one of the oldest manmade materials that has proven to stand the test of time. Each brick must be laid next to another brick to build a structure. Whether facilitating or making policy, this approach-

- Builds mutually respectful relationships

- Creates respected space for self-discovery processing

- Allows for ownership to take place

- Approaches courageous conversations through civil discourse

---

256 Ibid, 22.

- Seeks transformational changes

Lewis's philosophy is deeply rooted in Mahatma Gandhi and Rev. Martin Luther King Jr's civil advocacy approach. To be skilled in the BRIC Approach takes intrapersonal communication, interpersonal communication, intercultural communication, and endurance.

Lewis has created an awarding winning equity, diversity, and inclusion program, known as CEID – Cultural Excellence: Ideas and Discussions. The goal of CEID is to: **Achieve** operational excellence through cultural awareness, intercultural communication, and collegial collaborations. **Attain** inclusivity of the entire organization. **Build** the core of all employees to move with the organization on the cultural agility continuum.

Geneva Gay's work informed how CEID helped participants move from education to activation through:

- Self-discovery of blind spots within the organization

- Defining and understanding and building common cultural terms and definitions

- Self-assessment and discovery of personal cultural mindset

- Growth in cultural mind shifting

- Training in Reflective Equity Leadership

- System thinking and problem solving

Shanell Walter is a human resources officer in the United States Army, also known as the Adjutant General Corps. An officer in the Adjutant General Corps is an administrative officer who is responsible for the administration and preservation of personnel records.[257] In this role, she has worked with personnel to ensure that they understood the orders given to them. Understanding not everyone learns or relates

---

257 Adjutant general, "Merriam-Webster," accessed September 25, 2022, https://www.merriam-webster.com/dictionary/adjutant%20general.

the same way, Captain Walter demonstrated cultural care by connecting individuals to resources and support to help them accomplish the mission. Geneva Gay emphasizes the importance of cultural knowledge as one of the approaches to culturally responsive care. According to Lewis III and Garcia, military personnel and their families receive benefits, however with these benefits, "… however, with these benefits comes stressors to include "deployment of a parent to a warzone, frequent moves to new military bases –often leading to depression and sleep disorders as well as anxiety."[258]

During deployment, one of Captain Walter's roles was as a postmaster.[259] During deployment, was culturally responsive to the needs and care of her soldiers by assuring that information was directed and reached between soldiers and their families. With only one percent of the United States population in the military, family support and connection are key to mental, physical, and emotional health. Layered are the intersections of culture. Without specific care, understanding the ethos, and how to be culturally responsive, Captain Walter would not have been as successful in her roll.

Erika Lourenco de Freitas is an Assistant Dean for Equity, Diversity, and Inclusion at the University of Colorado Skaggs School of Pharmacy and Pharmaceutical Sciences. As a pharmacist, her job is to dispense prescription medications to patients. According to Stobierski, pharmacists "play an essential role in educating patients about using or administering their medications."[260] Stobierski goes on to say, "they serve as a "final check" to ensure that doses are correct and that patients will not experience negative or harmful drug interactions."[261] Lourenco de Freitas extends these responsibilities through using the tenets of Geneva Gay's work along with her research to

258 Charles E. Lewis III and Lynn Chandler Garcia, "The Black Military Family: Inspiring Through Military Legacy," *Black History Bulletin* 83, no. 2 (2020): 60.
259 Postmasters General, "U-S-History.com," accessed September 25, 2022, https://www.u-s-history.com/pages/h1233.html.

260 Tim Stobierski, "What Do Pharmacists Do? Roles and Responsibilities," *Northeastern University* (blog), January 3, 2022, https://www.northeastern.edu/graduate/blog/what-do-pharmacists-do/
261 Ibid, para. 4.

approach and treat her clients in equitable ways through culturally responsive health care services. From the beginning of the pandemic and the deep concerns around COVID-19, Lourenco de Freitas strategized ways to help mitigate historical medical concerns of people of color. She understood that many were facing, at a greater rate, "isolation, economic downturn, consequent job losses, financial instability, increased anxiety with the fear of contamination due to low income or public housing arrangements."[262] She too used Dr. Gay's five essential elements of culturally responsive teaching as an approach to care. Working with her staff, Lourenco de Freitas made sure they had an awareness of and addressed the mental health access disparities. This was the "foundational step for achieving health care equity."[263]

Next steps were to take action based on this awareness by examining the policies and systems that perpetuated these disparities within health care. Lourenco de Freitas explicitly provided resources to culturally competent mental health and wholistic health professionals to better assist patience in removing barriers as people of color when accessing care. "The literature suggests that [patients] achieve better outcomes and adhere to treatment when they have a provider who looks like them and can relate to psychological effects of racism."[264] In the classroom, as part of her intercultural care in instruction, Lourenco de Freitas expresses this to her students and teaches her students not only the standards as pharmacy technicians, but also the history of health care trauma for people of color. This leans itself to culturally inclusive classroom, relatability, and achievement of students of color. Ultimately, Lourenco de Freitas's work contributes to the increase of pharmacists of color who can and will serve and inform patients of color as well as all patients.

## Common Thread

---

262 Ericka Lourenco de Freitas, A. Franco, and A. Teasdell, "Black Mental Health Matters: Bridging the Mental Gap in the Black Community," *Black History Bulletin* 2 (2021): 20.
263 Ibid.
264 Ibid, 21.

Not knowing one another, we were all introduced to the works of Geneva Gay in college. One thing we all had in common was we all felt like reading her books and articles made us all feel like she knew us. She gave us the words to describe our experiences and how to articulate what we needed from our instructors. Gay's work became the framework of our undergraduate and graduate experiences. We had a guide even when support was not readily available.

So, who is Geneva Gay? We all have asked that question and wondered what it would be like to meet an icon of this work. In comparing our thoughts, we all were under the false impression that Gay was not accessible; someone whose scholarship was beyond our reach. This could not have been further from the truth; all of our experiences with this work were deeply enhanced once we personally and individually met Gay. In rooms filled with academics, historians, prolific writers, and scholars, she spoke to everyone as if she had known them, including the three of us. Gay knew how to navigate the room, differentiating without hierarchy. In every conversation and presentation, she demonstrated her work through her actions.

Through those experiences, all three of us: Educator and Entrepreneur, U.S. Army Captain, and Assistant Dean, though independent, our perspective and approach has made a united voice to guide others and inform policy, procedures, and practices.

# CHAPTER 7

# Using the Components of Culturally Responsive Teaching to Guide Education Reform

*By: María T. Colompos-Tohtsonie, Marisol Alonzo, & Courtney Carroll*

## Introduction

Schools throughout the United States are believed to be societal institutions that foster academic achievement and supportive learning environments. However, schools have very complex social settings or organizational environments and interpersonal relationships, which are varying social interactions between students and teachers.[265] Analyzing the school climate, which is the structural atmosphere and cultural ideologies of a school, provides an in depth understanding of the cultural variables that hinder or support the academic progression, physical safety, and social/emotional security of students.[266]

Historically, schools within the United States have not effectively produced a school climate that meets the needs of diverse populations who have varied values, languages, and social norms or collective behaviors linked to certain groups of people.[267] Involving minority

---

265 Lynn Kell Spradlin and Richard D. Parsons, Diversity Matters Understanding Diversity in Schools (Boston: Cengage Learning, 2008), 50.
266 Ibid, 48.
267 Ibid, 46.

families and communities in the school's mission and execution of that mission to educate their children is often difficult. "Only about 1 in 10 low-income and minority parents belong to parent-teacher organizations nationwide."[268] Further, schools are generally unaware of the changing demographics that limit time and availability of teachers and parents. Involving parents and educators to construct and reinforce the presentation of their perspectives in programming, curricula, policies, and practices will strengthen communication networks within the school environment.[269]

School climate data acknowledges student, parent, and school personnel concerns and assesses all the dimensions that shape the process of teaching and learning and educators' and students' experiences in the school environment. Understanding a school climate that offers low expectations and limited opportunities for academic success allows educators and policy practitioners to further examine the cultural lens, which are the opinions formed about particular social aspects of certain groups of people—between teachers and students. School climate data has shown to be beneficial in promoting meaningful educator, family, and student engagement and enhances the social, emotional, ethical, and intellectual skills that contribute to students' academic success. Moreover, schools need to invest more resources and time to examine whether they have integrated supportive learning environments, especially for minority and low-income students. As history has shown, the climate of a school sets the stage for encouraging or discouraging student motivation and achievement. Therefore, a direct intervention by educators, educational policy makers, and parental communities need to be placed at the forefront of all schools within the United States.

With this in mind, recognizing that human ecology, which involves the influential forces of the environment on human behavior can reveal internal pressures of institutional racism, where pervasive

268 Ibid, 54.
269 Ibid, 55.

social policies maintain the social advantage of the dominant racial group in school, sexism, classism, ableism, and heterosexism.[270] Educators and students regularly experience instances of incivility, such as uncivil mannerisms and qualities that negatively affect students' feelings of acceptance and productivity in schools.[271] As a result, most schools in the 1980s conducted cultural audits derived from Geneva Gay's culturally responsive teaching tenets, which examines the school's cultural characteristics such as institutional assumptions, customs, philosophical views, and values, to determine whether the existing cultural characteristics create a growth oriented student-centered school climate.[272]

In a school setting, understanding the climate of a school is crucial in following the educational mission of promoting favorable learning conditions and empowering all scholars. The key dimensions in establishing a positive school climate are safety, teaching and learning, interpersonal relationships, and institutional environment.[273] Each dimension has corresponding factors that must be adopted by schools to develop progressive learning environments.

Research within the sociocultural education discourse have identified that a sustained school climate boosts students' socioemotional development and academic achievement.[274] Additionally, the effects of school climate on learning have not been fully merged in contemporary school reform policies to include the No Child Left Behind Act, which resulted in the widening of the achievement gap between minority students and their counterparts.[275] When evaluating the school climate as a component that affects minority students, teachers must consider the degree of devaluation in a student's cultural

270 Ibid, 46.
271 Ibid, 47.
272 Ana María Villegas and Tamara Lucas, "The Culturally Responsive Teacher," Educational Leadership (2007):30.
273 Ibid, 31.
274 James A. Banks, "Failed Citizenship and Transformative Civic Education," Educational Researcher 46 no. 7 (2017): 370.
275 Lorraine M. McDonnell, "Educational Accountability and Policy Feedback," Educational Policy 27 no.1 (2012): 179.

and academic identity. Minority students who experience learning environments that neglect to reinforce their sociocultural perspectives are more likely to reject aspects of their culture and acculturate or relinquish customs linked to one's own culture of origin with the dominant culture.[276] When integrating the components of culturally responsive teaching within the school structure, these components must align with educational reform initiatives spearheaded by local and state educational leaders.

This chapter analyzes the ways in which each component of educational leadership policy is defined, how education policy impacts culturally responsive leadership, the integration of educational equity in formulating educational leadership policy, and the impact of governance and organizational political contexts within education reform.

## Educational Leadership Policy

Educational leadership policy is composed of visionary, culturally responsive, research-based, and data-driven approaches that are focused on bolstering learning environment quality mechanisms and academic management structures.[277] Educational leadership infuses practical processes to prepare teachers, counselors, administrators, superintendents, principals, and practitioners to work effectively within educational organizations.[278] Education systems are continually seeking ways to improve academic success of scholars through professional development, teaching processes, and classroom resources. A salient factor of educational leadership is adhering to policies within the federal, state, and local levels of educational governance and practice. Educational leadership policy is the blueprint for instilling critical debate and actions to advance policies and practices to make education more equitable in the lens of opportunity and academic

---

276 James A. Banks, "Failed Citizenship and Transformative Civic Education," 370.

277 William Black and Khaula Murtadha, "Toward a Signature Pedagogy in Educational Leadership Preparation and Program Assessment," Journal of Research on Leadership Education, 2 no. 1 (2007): 5.

278 Thomas A. Birkland, An Introduction to the Policy Process: Theories, Concepts, and Models of Public Policy Making (New York: Routledge, 2019).

outcomes.

## Components of Educational Leadership Policy

The components of educational leadership policy involve the efficiency of certain educational leadership styles and policy knowledge attainment of educational leaders. Educators come from diverse backgrounds and hold different leadership aspirations within different geopolitical educational spaces.[279] Tyack and Hansot defined educational leadership as: An understanding of, and the ability to guide and manage, appropriate resources, effective systems, and staff members and community resources that drive and support the educational endeavor—including those systems, people, and activities involved in policy-related work.[280]

As such, educational leadership involves different leadership styles to include strategic, adaptive, and transformational leadership. Strategic leadership focuses on educators who encourage a mind-set that will foster expedient change and innovative learning within the environmental conditions in their decision-making process. When educators exercise strategic leadership, they can create inclusive learning environments for scholars based on assessment protocols.

Adaptive leadership emphasizes how educators use available resecures to amplify technical innovation and learning techniques with a certain degree of implementation support from the education system.[281] The integration of adaptive leadership allows teachers to expand their knowledge networks to obtain teaching resources from the local and state educational agencies.[282] Moreover, transformational leadership outlines how educators apply new insights into classroom settings and make improvements in learning mechanisms based on

---

279 Jane Clark Lindle, "Ensuring the Capacity of University-Based Educational Leadership Preparation: The Collected Works of the National Commission for the Advancement of Educational Leadership Preparation," *Educational Administration Quarterly* 38, no. 2 (2002): 130.
280 David Tyack and Elisabeth Hansot, Mangers of Virtue: Public School Leadership in America, 1820-1980 (New York: Basic Books, 1982), 43.
281 Montgomery Van Wart, Leadership in Public Organizations (New York: Routledge, 2015).
282 Curry Stephenson Malott, Policy and Research in Education: A Critical Pedagogy for Educational Leadership (New York: Peter Lang 2010).

their own insights to generate creative solutions for different organizational education issues.[283] Educators demonstrate transformational leadership by inculcating productivity and collective efficacy among scholars through viable innovative teaching approaches to counteract ambiguous organization guidelines.[284] Leadership styles within educational leadership are contingent on the refined policy knowledge nexus of educational leaders.

Policy knowledge of educators is a crucial component in educational leadership policy as it helps educational leaders identify how school practices are molded by various system and non-system actors and respond to legal school requirements within the context of local and state educational agencies.[285] Educational policy has processes that form the school experience for educational leaders and expands their frames of reference on effectively navigating policy mechanisms, governance, and social norms.[286]

Education policy is the segway in converting educators into advocates for change who can positively affect policy outcomes and articulate the stewardship of the school learning paradigm.[287] Furthermore, education policy furthers the development of methods used by educational leaders for involving school stakeholders in the visioning and design of student assessment processes.[288]

## Culturally Responsive Leadership

Education policy contributes to leadership within education

283 Bernard M. Bass and Bruce J. Avolio, Improving Organizational Effectiveness through Transformational Leadership (Thousand Oaks: Sage Publications, 1994).

284 Peter G. Northouse, Leadership: Theory and Practice, 7th ed. (Washington, DC: Sage Publications, 2017).

285 Norris M. Haynes, Sousan Arafeh, and Cynthia McDaniels. Educational Leadership: Perspectives on preparation and practice (Lanham: University Press of America, 2014).

286 Steven I. Miller, "Defining Educational Policy Studies as a Field," Educational Studies 12, no. 2 (1981: 119–124.

287 James E. Anderson, Public Policymaking: An Introduction (Boston: Wadsworth/Cengage Learning, 2011).

288 Jane Clark Lindle, (2002). "Ensuring the Capacity of University-Based Educational Leadership Preparation: The Collected Works of the National Commission for the Advancement of Educational Leadership Preparation," Educational Administration Quarterly 38 no. 2 (2002): 129–137.

systems by enhancing the application of feasible solutions to address educational social problems.[289] Education policy is defined as, "a relatively stable, purposive course of action or inaction followed by an actor or set of actors in dealing with a problem or matter of concern."[290] Education policy imparts on leadership by helping educational leaders develop an applicable understanding of education policy fundamentals, practices, key stakeholders, and uses.[291] Additionally, education policy for educational leadership in a United States context illuminates the historic underpinnings of landmark education policies, main contributors of policy change, and uses of policy research in policy advocacy techniques.[292] When education policy is applied by educational leaders, they become more conversant with policy requirements, policy negotiation processes, and the unintended consequences of policy outcomes.[293]

The implementation of culturally responsive teaching molds inclusive classroom environments by concentrating on the strengths and abilities of each student and reduces adherence to deficit model thinking from others within the school structure.[294] It is salient that teachers within the education system examine their preconceived notions concerning diversity, needs, and expectations. Research conducted by Anyon[295] and Gay[296] have identified strong correlations between the quality of services provided to students who are culturally and/or linguistically diverse and the teacher's attitudes and expectations for these students. Therefore, culturally responsive classrooms

289 Joshua D. Clinton and Jason A. Grissom, "Public Information, Public Learning and Public Opinion: Democratic Accountability in Education Policy," Journal of Public Policy 35 no. 3(2015): 355–385.
290 James E. Anderson, Public Policymaking, 6.
291 Harold D. Lasswell, "The Policy Orientation," in The Policy Sciences: Recent Developments in Scope and Method, eds. Daniel Lerner and Harold D. Lasswell (Palo Alto: Stanford University Press, 1951), 3-15.
292 Robert B. Kottkamp, "Introduction: Leadership Preparation in Education," Educational Administration Quarterly 47 no. 1 (2010): 3–17.
293 Sandra J. Stein, The Culture of Education Policy (Thousand Oaks: Sage Publications, 2004).
294 Sharon R. Vaughn, Candace S. Bos, and Jeanne Shay Schumm, Teaching Exceptional, Diverse, and At Risk Students in the General Education Classroom (New York: Pearson, 2006).
295 Jean Anyon, Ghetto Schooling: A Political Economy of Urban Educational Reform (New York: Teacher's College Press, 1997).
296 Geneva Gay, Educational Equity for Students of Color (Boston: Allyn & Bacon, 2001).

reinforce educational structural inclusion by enhancing civic equality and academic engagement of students from culturally and/or linguistically diverse backgrounds.

Since educational leadership is primarily conducted through cultivated knowledge networks and collaboration with educators, parents, students, and policymakers, education policy must be ingrained in all facets of analytical and functional educational activities.[297] Education policy helps educational leaders conceptualize the inputs and outputs of policy actors such as legislative staff, state and local boards of education, interest groups and coalitions, and think tanks.[298] The trajectory of educational equity policy has become more imperative for school leaders as policy change is substantial and rapid throughout the United States.[299] The education policy directions have displayed significant need for educational leaders to adopt the equity values demarcated in newly distributed policies within education.[300]

## Educational Equity in Formulating Educational Leadership Policy

Equitable schools provide the climate, process, and content which allow students and educators to perform at their highest potential through educational leadership policy audits.[301] Since teaching is socially constructed, educators must understand the specifics of policy assurance and how teacher and student identities are formed in social settings.[302] Educational leadership policy audits ensure that schools adhere to equitable tenants by warranting successful academic outcomes through appropriate resources and instructional strategies for

---

297 Frank R. Baumgartner and Bryan D. Jones, "Agenda Dynamics and Policy Subsystems," Journal of Politics 53, no. 4 (1991): 1044–1074.
298 Frances Fowler, Policy Studies for Educational Leaders: An Introduction (Boston: Pearson, 2009).
299 Cecil Miskel and Wayne K. Hoy, Contemporary Issues in Educational Policy and School Outcomes (Charlotte: Information Age Publishing, 2006).
300 Thomas R. Dye, Top Down Policymaking (New York: Chatham House Publishers, 2001).
301 Michael Fullan, Al Bertani, and Joanne Quinn, "New Lessons for Districtwide Reform," Educational Leadership 61, no. 7 (2004): 42–47.
302 Lynn Spradlin, Diversity matters: Understanding Diversity in Schools, 2nd edition (Boston: Cengage Learning, 2011).

all scholars.[303] Policy audits concerning educational equity streamline educational leadership policy by creating the following: a clear mission statement including provisions to equitable universal design principles, an inclusive learning environment with multicultural exhibitions, an adequate space with the various socioeconomic, racial, ethnic, language, gender, and disability groups within the school community, and a partnership network with parents, professional communities, and civic organizations to enhance the curriculum and opportunities for all students.[304] Educators must deliver educational services in accordance with federal, state, and local guidelines to safeguard educational equity.[305] The legal parameters of providing an equitable education influence the actions of teachers, students, parents, and administrators.[306] Educational equity segments within American public school law is paramount in disseminating legal requirements and identifying gaps in educational leadership policy to produce changes to policy and practice.[307]

## Impact of Governance and Organizational Political Contexts

Educational leaders must recognize the governance edifices and the body politic associated with the education system within which they operate.[308] Brighouse, Ladd, Loeb, and Swift describe the political atmosphere within the educational realm as "political pressures that may limit the capacity to influence the production of some educational goods and may severely restrict the space for action in pursuit of distributive values."[309] Federal and state led educational policies

303 Joseph Murphy, "Preparation for the School Principalship: The United States Story," School Leadership & Management 18, no. 3 (1998): 359–372.
304 "Criteria for an Equitable School–Equity Audit," MAEC, Education, Equity, Excellence, accessed September 5, 2022, https://maec.org/resource/criteria-for-an-equitable-school-equity-audit/.
305 David Schimmel, Louis Fischer, and Leslie Stellman, School Law: What Every Educator Should Know (Upper Saddle River: Prentice Hall, 2007).
306 Kern Alexander and M. David Alexander, American Public School Law, 8th edition (Belmont: Wadsworth, 2011)
307 Michael W. LaMorte, School Law: Cases and Concepts. New York: Pearson, 2011).
308 David F. Labaree, "Public Goods, Private Goods: The American Struggle over Educational Goals," American Educational Research Journal 34, no. 1 (1997): 39–81.
309 Harry Brighouse, Helen F. Ladd, Susanna Loeb, and Adam Swift, "Educational Goods and Values: A Framework for Decision Makers," Theory and Research in Education, 14, no. 1 (2016):

create a governance structure with leadership from congress members, governors, mayors, chief state school officers, and other policymakers to produce specific accountability protocols that are applicable to state initiatives.[310] Since the governance leadership turn-over rate constantly changes, educational leadership policy mechanisms are adjusted to mirror organization political enterprises and funding imperatives.[311] The progression of educational leadership policy is contingent on the political motives for shifting control over education by some city and state politicians in local contexts of an elected board that can direct influence on mayoral decisions.[312]

Furthermore, federalism has evolved in education as shown by modifying the educational system's balance between centralized and decentralized governance with the intentions of improving accountability policies.[313] Gutmann stated that "democratic education defends decentralization and diversity among public and private schools not as ultimate ends but as means to their achieving educational ends."[314] Educational leaders function as vehicles of change through intensifying reform values within existing educational policies in collaboration with advocacy groups.[315] Additionally, policy enlightens educational leaders to create synergetic relationships between the local, state, and federal levels by streamlining policy alternatives to operational notions of equity.[316] Through educational leadership policy, school leaders can apply policy knowledge to act politically and contribute to social

---

17.

310 Paul Manna and Patrick McGuinn, Education Governance for the Twenty-First Century: Overcoming the Structural Barriers to School Reform (Washington D.C.: Brookings Institution Press, 2013).

311 Domingo Morel, Takeover: Race, Education, and American Democracy (New York: Oxford University Press, 2018).

312 Noel Epstein, Who's in Charge Here?: The Tangled Web of School Governance and *Policy* (Washington, D.C.: Brookings Institution Press, 2004).

313 Lorraine M. McDonnell, "Educational Accountability and Policy Feedback," Educational Policy, 27, no. 2 (2013): 170–189.

314 Amy Gutmann, Democratic Education (Princeton: Princeton University Press, 1999), 297.

315 Eamonn Callan, Creating Citizens: Political Education and Liberal Democracy (Oxford: Oxford University Press, 1997).

316 Douglass S. Reed, On Equal Terms: The Constitutional Politics of Educational Opportunity (Princeton: Princeton University Press, 2003).

justice values.[317]

## Conclusion

Thus, the components of educational leadership policy are integral in strengthening culturally responsive leadership techniques within education, increasing educational equity in the formulation of educational leadership policy, and understanding the impact of governance and organizational political contexts in education reform efforts. Educational policy practitioners continue to make decisions in the acquisition of educational goods.[318] Kingdon contextualizes the importance of educational leadership policy through which, "school leaders make important decisions countless times every day, but they do so within a wider policy context that itself reflects a particular view of the world."[319] As education systems become more complex, educational leadership policy that embodies the principles of culturally responsive teaching proves to be more relevant in hyper-political and sociocultural landscapes.[320] Education policy has transformed the educational leadership paradigm with wider educational aspirations by means of research to evaluate teaching strategies and practices in order to create robust culturally responsive educational leaders.

317 Helen F. Ladd and Douglas L. Lauen, "Status Versus Growth: The Distributional Effects of School Accountability Policies," Journal of Policy Analysis and Management 29, no. 3 (2010): 426–450.
318 Tim L. Mazzoni, "Analyzing State School Policymaking: An Arena Model," Educational Evaluation and Policy Analysis 13, no. 2 (1991):115–38.
319 John Kingdon, Agendas, Alternatives, and Public Policies, 2nd edition (New York: Pearson, 2010), 24.
320 Monica R. Brown, "Educating All Students: Creating Culturally Responsive Teachers, Classrooms, and Schools," Intervention in School and Clinic 43, no. 1 (2007): 57–62.

# Part IV

## The Impact of Culturally Responsive Teaching on Practice

# CHAPTER 8

# Culturally Responsive Mentorship, Faculty of Color, and the Importance of Community

*By Alicia L. Moore*

**Introduction:** While researching some primary and secondary source materials related to the scholarly works of Dr. Carter G. Woodson, I, once again, came across the following quote: "*The same educational process which inspires and stimulates the oppressor with the thought that he is everything and has accomplished everything worthwhile, depresses and crushes at the same time the spark of genius in the Negro by making him feel that his race does not amount to much and never will measure up to the standards of other peoples.*"[321] For me, this quote transcends time, and could have as easily been written today, as in 1933. The quote reminded me of Dr. Geneva Gay, Professor Emerita, University of Washington, who had been chosen to receive the Carter G. Woodson Scholars Medallion by the oldest African American organization in the nation dedicated to African Americans' lived experiences -- The Association for the Study of African American Life and History (ASALH). The medallion is presented to a scholar whose career is distinguished through at least a decade of research,

---

321 Carter G. Woodson. AZQuotes.com, Wind and Fly LTD, 2022. https://www.azquotes.com/quote/1055780, accessed October 1, 2022.

writing, and activism in the field of African American life and history. At that place in time Dr. Gay had, for over three decades, dedicated her life to scholarship, mentorship, and activism through her community-engaged service, as well as her preservice and in-service teacher training. In fact, she is known as a cultural architect who carved a niche for herself as a national leader through the recognition of her work on Culturally Responsive Teaching practices within James Banks'[322] Multicultural Education. Her work is lauded by prominent educational organizations that labor to distribute information about Black History that connects with and supports student achievement. As a consequence, young scholars of all races and ages have benefited from the implementation of culturally responsive pedagogy, and its tenets, within school curriculum, curricular materials, and through informed teacher behaviors, instructional strategies, and personal reflections. It was at this moment that I realized the importance and the urgency to formally share my gratitude for Dr. Gay by acknowledging her mentorship and her vast catalog of service to the field of education - service which has sparked the genius of many, including myself.

Specifically, the impact of her work has permeated every sector of the educational spectrum -- from grade schools, to post-secondary schools, to educator preparation programs, and beyond - even if those affected have not all realized it. From my own personal perspective, as a Black, female scholar living and working in Central Texas, not only did Dr. Gay's mentorship and scholarship influence my work as a former teacher and principal in a public school district, but it was a driving force in my graduate studies, and my current professional career as a university professor. To illustrate how important her work has been throughout my adult life, it is necessary for me to share the importance of developing a scholar identity, some challenges to mentorship for faculty of color (FOC), the importance of culturally

---

322 Gay, Geneva. Culturally Responsive Teaching : Theory, Research, and Practice. New York :Teachers College Press, 2018.

responsive mentoring, the contributions of other culturally responsive scholars, and my personal account of Dr. Gay's liberatory mentorship[323] as backdrops that will illustrate the influence of Dr. Gay's life's work.

### From Woodson to Gay: Developing a Scholar Identity

In an online series that examines Chapter 5 of an award-winning book titled, *Fugitive Pedagogy: Carter G. Woodson and the Art of Black Teaching* (Jarvis R. Givens, 2021), author and activist, Rann Miller, of Philly's 7th Ward, shared this synthesis of that chapter's content:

In addition to having a passion for teaching, a multifaceted set of skills to instruct children and knowledge of your content, teachers need both professional (and personal) support to be high performing in the classroom. This support comes in the form of mentoring and comradery. Throughout his career, Dr. Carter G. Woodson provided Black teachers with opportunities to receive both.[324]

This chapter synthesis, and the overall content of the aforementioned book, illustrate Dr. Woodson's thoughtful consideration of the need for Black mentors to create and share communal, safe spaces with Black educators. In fact, Dr. Woodson mentored many Black scholars in a time when predominantly white institutions (PWIs) would have given little acknowledgment or credence, if any at all, to the importance of the kinds of mentorship and professional growth opportunities that are essential for rising scholars of color. In Dr. Woodson's view, mentoring sets a path that encourages scholars of color to cultivate a diverse set of skills that will ultimately "spark the genius" in other Black intellectuals, including children, by affirming their identities. In a similar vein, Dr. Gay shared her passion for mentoring college students (white and black) and stated that, from her own perspective, her

323 Peter Leonard and Peter McLaren, eds. Paulo Freire: A Critical Encounter (Oxfordshire: Routledge, 2002).
324 Rann Miller, "Mentoring and Supporting Black Teachers is Professional Standard: A Review of Fugitive Pedagogy, Carter G. Woodson and the Art of Black Teaching," About Philly's 7th Ward (blog), July 28, 2022, https://phillys7thward.org/2022/07/mentoring-and-supporting-black-teachers-is-professional-standard-a-review-of-fugitive-pedagogy-carter-g-woodson-and-the-art-of-black-teaching-chapter-5/.

"greatest contribution is the number of graduate students [she had] been able to mentor at the College." She went on to share that she tried to "model and translate [her]theoretical notions [of Culturally Responsive Teaching] into her teaching . . . standing toe-to-toe with [her students] in the learning process.[325] Her long-standing goal has been for teachers to validate and affirm the identity of Black students through their expectations of students' success. Though Woodson and Gay's target audiences of mentees may have been in contrast, their goal of subverting oppressive counternarratives of black incompetence and failure, through the intentional role of liberatory mentorship, has ultimately cultivated and nurtured scholar identity in educators of color, and/or their students of color. Scholar Identity is a term coined by Gilman W. Whiting[326], and in this instance is attributed to the academic lives of black scholars of all ages and in various educational settings. As an example, for black school children, scholar identity may live in their understanding that being smart is "cool" versus being nerdish, and then can be observed in their subsequent, scholarly behaviors (i.e., they *perform* scholar identity). For black educators, specifically those working in institutions of higher education, it may live in their cultivation of an identity that reflects their achievements, degrees, teaching effectiveness, content expertise, and/or their ability to create an academic brand that explains and explores their professional identity. For instance, "scholar identity" was highlighted in an article written by Stephen Aguilar, who explained scholar identity as "areas of expertise, methodological inclination, interests, publications, research agenda, reputation and anything else that may be important in your field. Thus, your scholarly identity is multifaceted and (ideally) signals to anyone who researches your work (googles you), what you have done, what you are doing and what you can potentially do in

325 "Geneva Gay: A Legacy of Elevating Multicultural Education to Prominence," UW College of Education, July 7, 2020, https://education.uw.edu/news/geneva-gay-elevating-multicultural-education-prominence .
326 Gilman W. Whiting, "Promoting a Scholar Identity among African-American Males: Implications for Gifted Education," Gifted Education Psychology Press 20 no. 3 (2020): 2-6.

the future."[327] Scholar identity, then, is an academician's outward-facing professional reputation.

For me, having transitioned from teaching to serving as a school principal, and completing a doctorate in Special Education, landing a position as an Assistant Professor of Education at a university seemed par for the course. Yet, it was in this new space that I began to realize that there were some, inherent, challenges for faculty of color.[328] Some of these challenges included: (1) students questioning the validity of my credentials, (2) faculty from other departments attempting to decipher my "fit" in the department and university structure - this included questions such as "Where did you receive your degree?", "Did you already know [someone] in the department?", (3) faculty and administrator continuing to "forget" the extent of my content expertise in the discipline, and (4) the infliction of intermittent microaggressions[329] from students, staff, and other faculty. As I learned to navigate the campus power structures it became increasingly obvious that my scholar identity was going to have a significant impact on my career trajectory . . . and it needed to stand on its own. But, as a new academician, what was my own inward-facing reputation (my personal identity)? Who was I? Who was I as a scholar? Who was I as a black, woman of color? Who was I as a researcher? Who was I as a servant leader and teacher? Did it matter to anyone at the university? Would it be deemed irrelevant? Would it be acceptable to the gate-keepers who guarded the pearly tenure gates? These were questions that I had never ventured to ask myself, and no graduate professor or department chair had ever encouraged me to ask, reflect upon, or answer. There were so many questions, and no one at the university

---

327 Stephen J. Aguilar, "Shaping a Scholarly Identity that Helps You Do What You Want in Academe (opinion)," Inside Higher Ed, July 26, 2018, https://www.insidehighered.com/advice/2018/07/26/shaping-scholarly-identity-helps-you-do-what-you-want-academe-opinion .
328 Frank Tuitt,, Michele Hanna, Lisa M. Martinez, María del Carmen Salazar, and Rachel Griffin, "Teaching in the Line of Fire: Faculty of Color in the Academy." Thought & Action (2009): 65-74.
329 Derald Wing Sue, Sarah Alsaidi, Michael N. Awad, Elizabeth Glaeser, Cassandra Z. Calle, and Narolyn Mendez, "Disarming Racial Microaggressions: Microintervention Strategies for Targets, White Allies, and Bystanders," American Psychologist 74, no. 1 (2019): 128.

to field them; at least not without the possibility of being deemed ill-prepared for the academy. Yet, I kept teaching, engaging in service, researching, writing, and carefully crafting my scholar identity; but, I knew I needed assistance. I needed a mentor who would be cognizant of the challenges I had faced, and those I had yet to face. It was nearing time for tenure, and I was frightened.

## The Hill We Climb: Faculty of Color and the Barriers to Mentorship

Amanda Gorman, poet laureate, pronounced "that [w]e are striving to forge our union with purpose. To compose a country committed to all cultures, colors, characters, and conditions of man. And so, we lift our gaze, not to what stands between us, but what stands before us. We close the divide because we know to put our future first, we must first put our differences aside. We lay down our arms so we can reach out our arms to one another."[330] Through the lens of mentorship provided to us by Dr. Woodson, reaching out our arms to one another, in the context of his desire for African Americans to be mentored by other African Americans, could mean that we are continuing our work toward the dismantling of the vestiges of slavery and the psychological warfare of the oppressor, and nothing stands between us, or our community - in this case, our educational community. Yet, this union of purpose does not form without its challenges.

Though universities and institutions of higher education have existed in the United States for generations, and are staffed by multiple hundreds of faculty members, the face of many institutions still reflect an outdated, antiquated, and colorless system that does not reflect today's society - yet, they tout strong strategic plans chocked full of diversity initiatives to come.. In other words, as times have changed, the demographic landscape of the United States has also changed, which has presented many universities with a desire to make

---

330 Amanda Gorman, The Hill We Climb: An Inaugural Poem for the Country (New York: Viking Books, 2021).

a landscape change of their own.[331] The recruitment, hiring, and retention of diverse faculty is a tall order for many colleges. Faculty of color face advents of subtle workplace discrimination such as tokenism and being the recipients of outsized service obligations. This is why it is so important that the effective mentoring of all faculty, at any institution of higher education, be instrumental in developing a communal, safe, and open space in which new faculty members could thrive. However, within the overwhelmingly white demographic of PWIs, the ability for faculty of color (FOC) to thrive may take more than the usual institutional pairings of new faculty with senior faculty. Specifically, faculty of color may face a unique set of challenges during mentoring such as receiving little to no mentoring, being paired with a White mentor in which there is a cultural incongruency, experiencing cursory mentoring relationships, being mentored by a mentor who does not encourage, nurture, guide, and/or inspire the mentee to meet their career goals - a mentoring experience that does little to provide adequate support.

Zambrana, et al. examined the mentoring experiences of underrepresented minority faculty, found additional challenges to quality mentoring including "feeling neglected, experiencing a patchwork of mentors, and perceptions of limited understanding and limited acceptance of their research agenda[s]."[332] In a third study, published in the Journal of Career Development in 2021, one-hundred eighteen tenure-track FOC, at a research PWI, were interviewed about the barriers they faced as mentees.[333] The results of the study not only confirmed a demographic disparity, but also a major gender disparity, as well. Respectively, Latinx and Black women, considered "anti-intellectual",

331 Han, Insoon, and Jacqueline Ariri Onchwari, "Development and Implementation of a Culturally Responsive Mentoring Program for Faculty and Staff of Color," Interdisciplinary Journal of Partnership Studies 5, no. 2 (2018): 3.
332 Ruth Enid Zambrana, Rashawn Ray, Michelle M. Espino, Corinne Castro, Beth Douthirt Cohen, and Jennifer Eliason, "Don't Leave Us Behind: The Importance of Mentoring for Underrepresented Minority Faculty," American Educational Research Journal 52, no. 1 (2015): 40–72. https://doi.org/10.3102/0002831214563063
333 Tangier M. Davis, Martinque K. Jones, Isis H. Settles, and Paulette Granberry Russell, "Barriers to the Successful Mentoring of Faculty of Color," Journal of Career Development (2021): 08948453211013375.

also described their experiences as mentees as either woefully inadequate or there was no mentor present at all. These types of mentoring experiences may manifest themselves in particular ways based upon the respective circumstances affecting those tasked with mentoring FOC, such the utilization of untrained and/or inexperienced mentors, overworked FOC who were voluntold[334] to participate as diversity-focused mentors, differing/or conflicting personalities between mentor and mentee(s), and even mentors who are seeking information to further their own research goals. As a result of the findings of these studies, several recommendations were made for academic institutions. One study suggested the establishment of rigorous and deeply entrenched mentoring programs to prevent a potential downturn in staffing. Another focused on the creation of their own culturally responsive mentoring programs to combat such challenges to faculty of color. This mentoring program was implemented at the University of Minnesota's Duluth (UMD) campus in the form of a 2014 mentoring program. Like culturally responsive teaching, the culturally responsive mentoring program at UMD is oriented towards recognizing the strength in diversity to overcome challenges. The culturally responsive mentoring framework was entirely administered by faculty and staff of color and was immensely successful as evidenced by participants who credited the program's meetings and surveys with strengthening bonds with colleagues, thus creating a stronger sense of belonging on the campus. But, I am venturing to go a step further to recommend that, as Woodson espoused, FOC be paired with FOC at their institutions when the opportunity arises, and/or be paired with FOC from other, similar institutions.

## My Personal Mentoring Challenges:

While the experiences of faculty of color are not monolithic, there may be some shared experiences related to the barriers to mentoring that FOC mentees face on their respective campuses. In the wake of

334 Wiktionary contributors, "voluntold," Wiktionary, The Free Dictionary, accessed October 21, 2022, https://en.wiktionary.org/w/index.php?title=voluntold&oldid=43565577

the 2020 protests for racial justice, teaching about racism and multiculturalism has continued to be a battleground between educators and conservative state and federal officeholders. In Texas, the state's lieutenant governor, Dan Patrick, threatened to pass legislation through the conservative dominated Texas legislature that would punish professors who taught Critical Race Theory (CRT) or any other social justice content in their courses.[335] Infuriatingly, Culturally Responsive Teaching has become synonymous with Critical Race Theory and is seen as an erasure of whiteness, while rendering white students, including college students, disenfranchised. Similar threats against public universities have been issued by state officials in Florida, South Carolina, Mississippi, and other states which are led by conservative legislatures. With each passing day, the damage to the cultural climate and landscape, as a result of conservative culture wars against culturally responsive teaching, steadily erode the fundamentally equitable paths of inclusivity and the affirmation of positive black student identity. Likewise, university faculty, especially FOC, are now subject to harsh treatment and criticism, while also having to worry about potential barriers to tenure and promotion. As well, there may be impediments to teaching about their research, and/or teaching courses that disproportionately explore racial issues (the same can be said for issues relating to gender identity). The new crusade against culturally responsive teaching has elevated the need for universities to quickly form mentoring programs for members of their faculty[336]. The authors of the opinion piece in Inside Higher Ed "The Change Higher Education Needs Today" cooperated with their Faculty of Color Working Group to design a faculty mentoring approach that focused on communal aspects of mentoring, rather than individualistic configurations of mentoring. mentors and mentees, as described in the opinion piece, are strong cohorts in the system. Ideas, concepts, and works are exchanged and collaborated on during the various workshops that

335 Irene Mata, Melva Treviño, and M. Gabriela Torres, "The Change Higher Education Needs Today," Inside Higher Ed, May 13, 2022.
336 Ibid.

take the stead of mentoring sessions in order to prepare vast numbers of mentees to be unified in their indomitable sense to make transformative changes in the face of new waves of oppression.

## The Contributions of Culturally Responsive Mentors and Scholars

Culturally Responsive Mentoring refers to any form of education or teaching that incorporates the histories, texts, values, beliefs, and perspectives of people from different cultural backgrounds[337] while Culturally Responsive Teaching is similarly defined, by Dr. Gay, as "using the cultural knowledge, prior experiences, frames of reference and performance styles of ethnically diverse students to make learning encounters more relevant to and effective for them."[338] In Gay's seminal book titled, *Culturally Responsive Teaching: Theory Research, and Practice*, she linked the tenets of Dr. Woodson's work with that of James Banks' influential work in multicultural education, and Gloria Ladson-Billings[339] work in culturally relevant pedagogy. The combination of the work of these three brilliant scholars and champions of African American life, history and culture in schools, set a trajectory for expanding the reach of Gay and setting a course that would pay homage to Dr. Woodson's goal to honor the contributions of Black individuals through the teaching of other Black educators, while also educating them about their own cultural strengths. As well, Gay's emphasis on the outcomes of students of color, based upon the development of teaching strategies and curriculum that use students' cultural referents and strengths, translate into outcomes for educators of color, their scholar identity, and the impetus for igniting their "sparks of genius".

---

337 "Multicultural Education," The Glossary of Education Reform, accessed October 20, 2022, https://www.edglossary.org/?s=multicultural+education.

338 Gay Geneva, Culturally Responsive Teaching: Theory, Research, and Practice (New York, Teachers College Press, 2018), 31

339 Gloria Ladson-Billings,"Toward a Theory of Culturally Relevant Pedagogy," American Educational Research Journal 32, no. 3 (1995): 465-491.

## Did Culturally Responsive Mentorship Save My Academic Life?

Though I should not have been surprised, talking to my students (many of whom were prospective teachers) about race and culture was much more difficult than I had originally anticipated. I was well aware that at predominantly white institutions (PWIs) across the country, when faculty of color teach courses that delve into race, culture, ethnicity, etc. it usually involves asking students who do not identify as being "of color" to look at themselves or their behaviors closely. These students are asked to examine their biases, the stereotypes they hold for those who do not look, sound, or speak the way they do, and ways in which these things may impact their students, specifically their students of color.[340] In fact, I had personally been a witness to several college classroom discussions that encouraged White, prospective teachers to engage in an exploration of history, statistics about gaps in student achievement, and teacher biases which lead to resistance and angst rather than an analysis of causal relationships that served as barriers to student success. Similarly, as a new faculty member in the department of education, I could not initially lecture about or discuss white privilege.[341] In one course (*Schools, Society, and Diversity*) I was tacitly dared to discuss race or diversity as main topics of discussion, and conversations about systemic racism and structures of power, privilege and oppression seemed to be powder kegs filled with explosive defensiveness, and misinformation sprinkled with anger - they could not fathom that they were being asked to step outside of their comfortable culturally and racially-insulated bubbles. But I, on the other hand, certainly had to be examined under a microscope and questioned about my curricular motives as I bear in the familiar distaste of white fragility[342] and fatigue.[343] I believe that my early

340 Beverly Tatum, "Talking about Race, Learning about Racism: The Application of Racial Identity Development Theory in the Classroom," Harvard Educational Review 62, no. 1 (1992): 1-25.
341 Derald Wing Sue, David P. Rivera, Nicole L. Watkins, Rachel H. Kim, Suah Kim, and Chantea D. Williams, "Racial Dialogues: Challenges Faculty of Color Face in the Classroom." Cultural Diversity and Ethnic Minority Psychology 17, no. 3 (2011):331-340.
342 Robin DiAngelo, White Fragility: Why it's so Hard for White People to Talk about Racism (Boston: Beacon Press, 2018).
343 Joseph E. Flynn, White Fatigue: Rethinking Resistance for Social Justice (New York: Peter

acquaintance with Culturally Responsive Pedagogy may have saved my academic life (and hopefully the academic and personal lives of school children and college students of color across the nation). As a new professor in the department of Education, I knew that Dr. Geneva Gay's seminal Culturally Responsive Teaching tenets and strategies would be threads woven throughout all of my courses and I set out on a trek to strengthen and enhance their collective mantras of "meeting the needs of ALL students" and "ALL students can learn". But, what I did not realize was that tenets embedded in Dr. Gay's work, though invaluable within elementary, middle, and high schools, were also necessary to ensure my survival (both emotionally and professionally). As a faculty member of color in a predominantly and persistently white, sometimes inhospitable, institutions of higher education the pillars of culturally responsive teaching **supported** my scholar identity, and laid bare the hegemonic structures in place that made that space intermittently untenable. In case you were wondering, I did receive tenure, thanks to the mentoring of Dr. Geneva Gay, not only as a personal mentor, but also and through her contributions to the field of education.

### The Power of Mentors like Dr. Gay:

Part of the college experience is establishing bonds. To bond is to make connections between students, professors, mentors, and on-campus organizations.[344] Founding new networks of friendship and collegiality are instrumental in crafting the sense of belonging that many need to grow into in order to feel truly at home. Faculty members, especially new FOC, are no exception. Mentoring methods can vary from institution to institution, yet one of the most effective means of mentoring is pairing a mentee with a mentor who shares the same ethnicity as the mentee. Oftentimes, as has been shared

Lang, 2018).
344 Annmarie Cano, "The Power of Academic Role Models 'Like Me'" Spark: Elevating Scholarship on Social Issues, July 11, 2019, https://medium.com/national-center-for-institutional-diversity/the-power-of-academic-role-models-like-me-7f4f2c59279d.

previously, faculty of color either do not have mentors or have mentors that do not profoundly impact their professional growth. When a mentee is matched with a mentor of the same ethnicity, the result is a huge morale boost for the mentee who will see their mentor as so much more than a mentor. The mentor is a role model in this relationship. The mentor, by their presence and experiences as a person of color, demonstrates to the mentee that they can succeed too. It is the mentee's "Carpe Diem moment" as evidenced in Annmarie Cano's personal essay in the National Center for Institutional Diversity titled "The Power of Academic Role Models "Like Me." Though her essay reflected her experiences working with students of color, the same benefits from effective and consistent mentoring can be transferred to the mentoring to university faculty of color.

Dr. Geneva Gay's service as a mentor can be seen in Dr. Carter G. Woodson's prolific scholarship and in his mentorship of younger scholars. Through his mentorship, his vision for an America that recognizes not only those who bore the hope and the dream of the slave[345], but also recognizes those whose contributions have served as threads in a garment of nation building, could continue to bring his vision to fruition. In like fashion, Dr. Gay has touched the lives of many teachers of history, to social studies, and those who promote and dedicate their lives to Multicultural Education, Culturally Responsive Teaching, through her mentorship. As a mentee of Dr. Gay, I, as a Co-Editor of the Association for the Study of African American Life and History's Black History Bulletin (BHB), use the framework of Culturally Responsive Teaching to scaffold the BHB content that is published in an effort to provide articles and lesson plans that teach students about African American History, life, and culture. As well, we have studied her, studied her work, and studied with her. In fact, my success is the measure of her long-standing success: Dr. Alicia L. Moore, Cargill Endowed Professor. She stands, not alone, but as a "we", reaching out to share her wisdom in a powerful, yet unassuming manner. Dr.

345 Maya Angelou, And Still I Rise: A Book of Poems (New York: Random House, 1978).

Gay has never failed to provide guidance and insights to me related to her historical knowledge of the backdrop of the contributions of African Americans in our nation. Dr. Woodson shared that, "[t]he real servant of the people must live among them, think with them, feel for them, and die for them." As a mentor to countless scholars from many disciplines, Dr. Gay has certainly never shied away from living among us, thinking with us, feeling for us (including children, mentees and educators} and, through her research, writing, and activism, she has shown proof that she will leave a legacy that follows in the footsteps of Dr. Carter Godwin Woodson – a legacy that serves to ensure a firm foundation for the continuance of African-centered education through the dedication and commitment to [accurate] African American history and ardent commitment to examine and confront issues that negatively impact African American children in their classrooms by using African American history to affirm their identities.

Dr. Gay's academic credentials, background and experience as a scholar, mentor, researcher, and historian leave an amazing legacy. But perhaps, even more importantly, though now retired, it should be noted that through her work, she has exhibited a deep commitment to continuously integrating, improving and building on culturally responsive teaching and mentoring as a strategy for preparing white practicing and pre-professional teachers to recognize the humanity in our children while teaching them their history, and in ourselves as university scholars. With this chapter, I honor Dr. Geneva Gay and thank her for the opportunity to study under tutelage as a mentee who has found her scholar identity.

**Author's Notes:**

- The American Association of Colleges and Universities (AAC&U) winner of the Frederic W. Ness Book Award is, *Fugitive Pedagogy: Carter G. Woodson and the Art of Black Teaching*, published by Harvard University Press. The Ness award is given annually to the book that best illuminates the goals and practices of a contemporary liberal education, and will be formally presented to the author, Jarvis R. Givens. Givens is an assistant professor at the Harvard Graduate School of Education and a faculty affiliate in the Department of African & African American Studies at Harvard University.

- The usage of the term, faculty of color (FOC) refers to faculty who self-identify as African-American or Black.

- The use of the terms, teacher, and professor, are subsumed under the term educator where appropriate.

# CHAPTER 9

# Geneva Gay and My Evolving Praxis of Culturally Responsive Computational Journalism Education

*By Kim Pearson*

At first glance, one could be forgiven for wondering what an undergraduate journalism educator who has never taught K-12 classes and who has no formal training in the discipline could contribute to a volume on the work of a major theorist in culturally responsive teaching in the K-12 classroom. If you put the proposition to me 25 years ago, I would have been skeptical myself. At that time, I was a newly-tenured teacher of journalism and professional writing teaching courses in feature and magazine journalism, public relations writing and the like. In my classes, I created virtual enterprises that mimicked the challenges my students would face in their professional lives and then showed them how to use the didactic content of those courses to meet those challenges.

My approach came intuitively and organically from reflecting on my own educational experiences and observations of my peers, alongside some scant exposure to educational philosophy that I will explain in more detail below. What Geneva Gay ultimately gave me was the language to understand the strategy that I had been groping for. I referred to myself as a constructivist pedagogue, but Geneva Gay helped me understand that I was also trying to discern a praxis of culturally responsive journalism education that would prepare students from diverse backgrounds to be effective, ethical and reflective leaders of an industry undergoing fundamental changes that could determine the future of democracy.

What's more, as I read the work of colleagues in journalism, computer science and the social sciences who were also engaged in pedagogical research in their own disciplines, I found Geneva Gay's name and ideas in their literature reviews and footnotes. When I finally read Dr. Gay's work and heard her speak, it was as if I finally had a name and face to attach to a voice I had been straining to hear for many years.

In this essay, I want to delineate the ways in which Dr. Gay's work helped me think through my own experiences, and how it helps guide my current work centered on fostering interdisciplinary, community-engaged academic collaborations that address real problems deepening students' scientific literacy and civic awareness.

Being mindful of what Dr. Gay refers to as "the nature of and need for story,"[346] I begin at my own beginning, as a Black child of the Sputnik generation. The 1957 launch of the Soviet Sputnik satellite ignited an all-out campaign to boost science education in United States' schools. It was the era of Kennedy's New Frontier, Martin's Dream, Malcolm's nightmare. It was the era of anticolonial revolution and the dawn of neocolonial reaction. In our textbooks and the mass media, we were shown visions of a space-age future. But save for Lt. Uhura in Star Trek, the people making that future didn't look like us.

In Philadelphia, where I began first grade in 1963, the man who had controlled the school district's finances since the 1920s, Add Anderson, had just retired. According to scholars, he was more interested in keeping property taxes low than he was in supporting public

346 Gay, Geneva. 2000. Culturally Responsive Teaching : Theory, Research, and Practice. Multicultural Education Series. New York: Teachers College Press. https://search.ebscohost.com/login.aspx?direct=true&db=nlebk&AN=34561&site=ehost-live.p.2

education. Author Peter Binzen called him, "a penny pincher all his life...a ruthless man filled with contempt for 'educators.'"[347] Although the district schools had been legally integrated since 1881, they were functionally segregated: black students were consistently assigned to the most dilapidated schools and fewer resources were directed to those schools. Tracking systems within schools led to black students being disproportionately assigned to "RE" (retarded educable) classes. Scholar Lisa Levenstein recalls a 1960 *Philadelphia Bulletin* series titled, "The Slow Learners," in which school superintendent Allen Wetter blamed black children for their plight, calling the children of the Great Migration "culturally deprived slow learners." The series referred to these "slow learners" as "unlovable characters" responsible for "a tragic deterioration of our schools."[348]

Dr. Gay's 2008 article for Education Digest about the consequences of the failure to implement culturally responsive teaching strategies to address the needs of roughly 500,000 children displaced by Hurricane Katrina makes an observation that could easily have been applied to the children and grandchildren of the Great Migration in Philadelphia and other cities:

> *"How were they to make a place for themselves in the midst of strangers, especially if their teachers and school principals were not providing guidance in making the transitions?*[349] "

Then again, how could those school leaders provide that guidance if all they saw was an undifferentiated mass of "culturally deprived," "unlovable" children? At the same time, as Dr. Gay reminds us,

> *"The individuality of students is deeply entwined with their ethnic identity and cultural socialization. Teachers need to understand very thoroughly both the relationships and the*

---

347 Paul Lyons, The people of this generation: The rise and fall of the New Left in Philadelphia. Philadelphia: University of Pennsylvania press, 2003. p. 15; and Lisa Levenstein, A Movement Without Marches: African American Women and the Politics of Poverty in Postwar Philadelphia UNC Press, April, 2009. p. 125.
348 Levenstein, p. 137
349 Gay, Geneva. "Teaching Children of Catastrophe." Education Digest 73, no. 9 (May 2008): 40–44. https://search.ebscohost.com/login.aspx?direct=true&db=aph&AN=32135603&site=e-host-live.

*distinctions between these to avoid compromising the very thing they are most concerned about—that is, students' individuality. Inability to make distinctions among ethnicity, culture, and individuality increases the risk that teachers will impose their notions on ethnically different students, insult their cultural heritages, or ignore them entirely in the instructional process. In reality, ethnicity and culture are significant filters through which one's individuality is made manifest. Yet individuality, culture, and ethnicity are not synonymous.*[350]

Fortunately, there were parents, civic leaders and activists who fought for our educational rights, and who saw the full range of our humanity. The Northern Freedom Movement gained momentum in Philadelphia during those years. There were the Black teachers in my segregated elementary school who told us about African kingdoms and urged us to do well for our people's sake. They saw my potential and worked with my parents to get me into Masterman, a laboratory and demonstration middle school established in 1958 through a bequest from its namesake, Julia Reynolds Masterman, to benefit city students who were considered to be gifted. There was Allan Wetter's integration-minded successor as Superintendent, Mark Shedd, who abolished IQ tests, integrated teaching staffs and funded innovative projects to boost student achievement. The city's high schools got its first Black teacher around the time I was born - Mary Elizabeth Henderson Wright. By the time I met her in 1971, she'd earned a doctorate and was serving as the first Black (and most formidable) vice principal of the Philadelphia High School for Girls[351] - the city's public high school for gifted girls that boasts a who's who of distinguished graduates.

There was my own father who learned from his coworkers at the Post Office that his GI benefits would pay for him to go to school,

350 Gay, Geneva. Culturally Responsive Teaching : Theory, Research, and Practice. Teachers College Press, 2000. p.23

351 House resolution HRO768 94 General Assembly, State of Illinois https://bit.ly/3UBPX4L

leading him to Temple University's high school program where he earned his diploma. By the time I entered Masterman at the end of fourth grade, he had nearly attained a dual bachelor's degree in education and accounting and was beginning graduate school. His career as a school teacher and administrator lasted nearly 30 years. His way of spending time with me was to make me his model student at the age of eight and beginning at age 10, his occasional research assistant. This was how I was exposed to various philosophies of education -Locke, Dewey, Piaget, Mill, Gardner. Rousseau's Emile and AS Neil's Summerhill reminded me of Masterman and fired my imagination. He took me to the storefront alternative program that he and the dashiki-wearing principal of Gratz High, Marcus Foster, created to keep pregnant students in school. We read and discussed Plato, Baldwin, Giovanni, King, Malcolm and Bertrand Russell. He sent me to Temple University library's microfilm collection to read Du Bois' Crisis. He taught me chess. He and my stepmother encouraged my interest in writing with Saturday morning and summer classes.

By the time I was finishing Girls High and heading to Princeton, he was writing his dissertation proposal while working a day job, two after-school jobs, and raising my brother. My stepmother was working the overnight shift in the mailroom of the Spiegel catalog company to help pay tuition for me and for my brother's private school.

At Masterman, I contributed to a class newspaper, wrote electronic music on graph paper, and learned to write a couple of simple programs in BASIC. At home, I kept journals about NASA space flights, played with my chemistry set, collected rocks and loved the Saturday morning meteorology class my parents found me. These were normal things for a Masterman kid.

Girls High, which also gave me many good things, didn't have a programming class for someone who wanted to program the one computer in the basement. I would go there and run the one program I knew. But the faculty who knew me affirmed me as a thinker and writer and nudged me toward the Ivy League schools that were just opening their doors to women - places they, themselves did not know.

Princeton also gave me many good things while also engendering puzzlement and frustration. I lost points on assignments for not understanding how much longer short-answer and essay responses should be than they had been in high school, for example. I took an elective calculus class and learned despite its 101 designation, it was designed for students who had taken the subject in prep school. When I consulted the library for my junior research paper, a policy analysis of the federal Minority Small Business Enterprise program, I was confused that the canonical sources said Black people didn't have a tradition of entrepreneurship. Now I understand that these so-called experts were either ignorant or dismissive of work of Black scholars and journalists documenting that history. Reflecting on the 50th anniversary of the Brown v. Board of Education Supreme Court decision, Dr. Gay captured the alienation and survivors' guilt many of us felt as Black students in predominantly White universities:

> *"To claim the promises made we left community and culture behind. And immersed ourselves in places and programs entirely Eurocentric in kind. Benefactors of this dubious progress are far too few. And, what about the many, many others whom some major changes are still due?"*[352]

Mentoring from Black graduate students, punishing solo study sessions, African American Studies courses and culturally-focused student organizations and media gave me the intellectual and psychological space to breathe and explore the answers to the questions that would help me figure out what my life's work would be. The University allowed students to come up with ideas for seminars, recruit a faculty member to teach them, and then obtain administration approval. We created several classes this way - one of my favorites was Cross-Cultural Perspectives on the Asian American Experience. Here, too, I began to explore journalism, co-founding a newsletter that became

[352] Geneva Gay (2004) The Paradoxical Aftermath of Brown, Multicultural Perspectives, 6:4, 12-17, DOI: 10.1207/s15327892mcp0604_5

a magazine and occasionally writing for the school newspaper. These experiences of being able to work with other students and supportive faculty and staff to create learning experiences rooted in our epistemologies, ontologies and burning questions stayed with me.

After college, a job as an information specialist at a comprehensive cancer center served as my introduction to health communications, media relations, and community engagement. That was followed by graduate school in journalism at New York University where I focused on science journalism. My goal was to make it to the New York Times science desk. There were four Black students in my cohort of 45, and only two of us made it past the second semester. The faculty awarded me a teaching assistantship that paid my tuition. I helped run a summer high school journalism workshop and volunteered with Youth Communications, a pioneering high school newspaper program. At the end of the summer workshop, the high schoolers presented me with a new briefcase and told me I should teach. ABC News anchor Ted Koppel presented me with a science writing award. Chuck Stone, one of the nation's most eminent Black journalists and a co-founder of the nascent National Association of Black Journalists, presented me with a list of openings in the Knight-Ridder chain.

But I didn't know how to talk to my professors and would-be mentors about the feelings that lingered from the racist verbal attack I experienced while covering my first election night story. I was sexually harassed and assaulted while trying to do an immersive reporting project for my magazine writing class and I didn't know what to do with the shame and rage I felt. It showed up in the writing, though, and when I workshopped my piece, my White classmates asked me what had happened. I froze, disappeared from class and put my revisions in my professor's mailbox. I didn't tell her what happened until about ten years ago. It's only in the last 20 years that journalists have been more open about the need for attention to the trauma that can come with the job. As a Black woman, I felt the pressure to suck it up. I would learn that a lot of journalists of color had far worse stories than mine - especially among women and queer colleagues.

So I didn't apply for the newspaper jobs - which didn't pay enough for me to buy the car I would have needed or pay back my student loans. I took a job as a writer for Bell Laboratories, the vaunted research and development arm of AT&T during the 1980s. There, I gained a sense of the ways in which what we now call the Internet would transform how we create, disseminate and interact with media. Indeed, as a public relations manager for them, I was responsible for helping to sell the utopian ideals of family, community life and civic possibility that these technologies might help us create. I also supported company executives who participated in the debates among policymakers, legislators, philanthropists and other thought leaders over the most effective and equitable ways to develop the workforce the country would need to thrive in the information economy. I supervised interns. I read the research on workforce preparedness. I talked to friends and colleagues in academia and came to the conclusion that I could help prepare students - and perhaps their teachers - for the world to come.

This is how I came to teach at a predominately White comprehensive state college in central New Jersey, where I still work more than three decades later. My approach in my classes was to simulate the real work world as much as possible. The professional writing students did public relations work for real clients. I had the magazine writing students create a real magazine with a real business plan that we pitched for real advertisers. Alumni donations and sweat equity helped us get four issues printed. Joined by like-minded colleagues in art, graphic design and communications, our students created ad campaigns that performed well in national competitions and many went on to great careers.

With colleagues in the art department, my magazine writing class launched our online news magazine, Unbound, in 1996. In journalism education jargon, Unbound was a lab publication. It ran continuously until 2008. I started having my students learn about the scripting languages of the web: html, then css and JavaScript. Today, that includes an introduction to creating virtual and augmented reality content as well. We also brought data journalism into the curriculum, making it a requirement in 2002.

It became clear that we had to have a more systematic approach to infusing computer science literacy into an already crowded curriculum. With colleagues in computer science and art, I helped found a program in Interactive Multimedia that began in 2003. My computer science colleague brought me in on a proposal to the National Science Foundation to engage middle schoolers in computing as a creative activity. Our interactive journalism institute for middle schoolers[353] attracted the attention of Dr. La Vonne I. Neal, and that was how I began conducting teacher workshops on using the Scratch programming language to teach computational thinking across the middle school curriculum. (Computational thinking is a problem-solving strategy focused on optimizing the combined capabilities of humans and computers.[354])

But computer science educators were struggling as much as journalism educators when it came to strategies for inclusive and equitable pedagogy, if not more. Jane Margolis' 2008 book, *Stuck in the Shallow End*[355] (MIT Press) exposed the unequal access to computer science education in the Los Angeles Unified School District and it didn't take long to recognize that this was a microcosm of a much larger problem. Some of us were also reading Bob Moses' book, Radical Equations, in which the co-creator of Freedom Summer explained how his Algebra project applied the Freedom Movement's strategies for teaching Black voters who were disenfranchised how to pass literacy tests. And many of us also turned to Geneva Gay, James Banks and their colleagues.

Scholarship on culturally responsive teaching and practice in computer science has grown in recent years. For example, Kimberly A.

353 Archived IJIMS home page. Some links have expired.: https://web.archive.org/web/20091123070831/https://www.tcnj.edu/~ijims/
354 Jeannette Wing. Computational Thinking: What and Why? (2010) https://www.cs.cmu.edu/~CompThink/resources/TheLinkWing.pdf
355 Margolis, Jane. Stuck in the Shallow End : Education, Race, and Computing. Cambridge, Mass. :MIT Press, 2008.

Scott, et. al, write of the development of "culturally responsive computing", which they describe" as an approach to devising technology supports and computer education programs informed by the extensive work in culturally responsive teaching.[356] Culturally responsive computing is similar to culturally responsive teaching in its emphasis on reflection, viewing students' cultures and community through an asset-based lens, and community building. They build upon culturally responsive teaching developing strategies to improve diverse students' learning experiences bridge students' cultures with STEM practices, and ensure that these culturally sustaining practices meet curricular needs.

David James cites Dr. Gay's advocacy for embedding "students' culture in their course materials, so students can use their own materials to understand concepts."[357] Elizabeth Reyes-Aceytuno's study of teachers' attitudes toward culturally responsive teaching found receptiveness to the principles of culturally responsive teaching, but complaints about the lack of time and resources to implement its practices.[358] Michael Lachney is another contributor to the group of young scholars focused on issues of equity in the development and deployment of educational technology in K-12 settings. His 2017 article, "Computational communities: African American cultural capital in computer science education:

> *"[E]xamines two ways that African-American cultural capital and computing can be bridged in CS education. The first is community representation, using cultural capital to highlight*

356 Kimberly A. Scott, Kimberly M. Sheridan & Kevin Clark (2015) Culturally responsive computing: a theory revisited, Learning, Media and Technology, 40:4, 412-436, DOI: 10.1080/17439884.2014.924966

357 David James. 2020. The Use of DJing Tasks as a Pedagogical Bridge to Learning Data Structures. In Proceedings of the 2020 ACM Conference on Innovation and Technology in Computer Science Education (ITiCSE '20). Association for Computing Machinery, New York, NY, USA, 193–197. https://doi.org/10.1145/3341525.3387427

358 Elizabeth Reyes-Aceytuno, Barbara Howard, and Staci Ma. 2020. Culturally Responsive Teaching Practice as It Relates to Teachers' Perspectives,. Ph.D. Dissertation. Concordia University Irvine. Advisor(s) Quiroz, Blanca. Order Number: AAI28022950.

*students' social identities and networks through computational thinking. The second, computational integration, locates computation in cultural capital itself. I survey two risks – the appearance of shallow computing and the reproduction of assimilationist logics – that may arise when constructing one bridge without the other. To avoid these risks, I introduce the concept of computational communities by exploring areas in CS education that employ both strategies. This concept is then grounded in qualitative data from an after school program that connected CS to African-American cosmetology"[359].*

Not surprisingly, James Davis, Michael Lachney, et. al. cite *Culturally Responsive Teaching* in their 2019 research article for the Special Interest Group on Computer Science Education, "A Cultural Computing Curriculum."[360]

Beginning with the aforementioned 2001-2010 Interactive Journalism Institute for Middle Schoolers (IJIMS) project (NSF Award #0739173), my colleagues and I have been exploring testing and refining models for deepening engagement with computational thinking and STEM literacy more broadly through the use of interdisciplinary, community-engaged collaborations. The IJIMS project engaged middle school learners and their teachers in computing by teaching them how to conceive and execute multimedia and interactive journalism projects. As Principal Investigator Ursula Wolz liked to put it, we sought to exploit the isomorphism between the process of software production and editorial production. Aligning with the principles of culturally responsive computing, we enlisted the teachers and students as collaborators in the process of designing the schedule

359 Michael Lachney (2017) Computational communities: African-American cultural capital in computer science education, Computer Science Education, 27:3-4, 175-196, DOI: 10.1080/08993408.2018.1429062

360 James Davis, Michael Lachney, Zoe Zatz, William Babbitt, and Ron Eglash. 2019. A Cultural Computing Curriculum. In Proceedings of the 50th ACM Technical Symposium on Computer Science Education (SIGCSE '19). Association for Computing Machinery, New York, NY, USA, 1171–1175. https://doi.org/10.1145/3287324.3287439

and activities for the institute.[361] Eventually, teachers and parents at the Middle School turned IJIMS into their school newspaper.

On the 2008-2012 project, Distributed Expertise in Computing With Connections to the Arts (NSF Award , journalism was one of the collaborating disciplines used to test our models for interdisciplinary classroom-based computing collaborations.[362] For my part, this included a three -part collaboration between a software engineering class at Villanova University, a game production class at The College of New Jersey, and my Interactive Storytelling class. The idea was to structure a collaboration around projects shared among classes with separate instructors and deliverables. The game production class gave my Interactive Storytelling class their "story bible" - a summary of characters and plot points. We analyzed the story for holes before they committed it to code. They also gave us two dynamic storytelling engines - one in Scratch and the other in Processing - that students could use to create their midterm projects. The students then had the option of sharing their interactive stories with the Villanova Software Engineering class to do a code review. At Howard University, faculty members in journalism and computer science teamed up to have students collaborate on producing News Games using our model. The project design aligned with the Culturally Responsive Computing principle that all students can be technology innovators, not just consumers.

Between 2012 and 2017, I joined my fellow Co-PI from the IJIMS project, Sarah Monisha Pulimodd to launch Collaborating Across Boundaries to Engage Undergraduates in Computational Thinking (CABECT) supported by NSF Award #1141170. We built on the cooperative expertise model of having two classes work together

361 Ursula Wolz, Meredith Stone, Kim Pearson, Sarah Monisha Pulimood, and Mary Switzer. 2011. Computational Thinking and Expository Writing in the Middle School. ACM Trans. Comput. Educ. 11, 2, Article 9 (July 2011), 22 pages. https://doi.org/10.1145/1993069.1993073

362 Thomas Way, Lillian Cassel, Kim Pearson, Ursula Wolz, Deborah Tatar, Steve Harrison. "A Distributed Expertise Model for Teaching Computing Across Disciplines and Institutions", 09/01/2009-08/31/2010, 2010, "Conference proceedings of The 2010 International Conference on Frontiers in Education: Computer Science and Computer Engineering (FECS 2010)".

on an interdisciplinary computing project with separate instructors and deliverables by having students work in cross-class teams with a community partner. The project was to have the students assist the community partner, Habitat for Humanity, with their need for better information about potential pollutants in properties they were considering acquiring for the purpose of building affordable housing. The idea was to involve all students in all phases of the design and development process, either in a leading or supportive role. By bringing together students with different disciplinary backgrounds and cultural perspectives, we hoped to engender creative solutions that deepened the non-STEM students' engagement with technology and enhanced the STEM students' communications, collaboration, and civic engagement.[363]

Since 2019, Dr. Pulimood, myself, and co-PI Diane Bates have expanded our Collaborating Across Boundaries model across our campus, and across the range of STEM and non-STEM disciplines. (NSF Award #194869) More than a dozen collaborations have been fostered under this grant including sociology students collaborating with nursing students to help a federally-qualified nursing staff community health center better serve their clients; computer science students working with criminology students to help a nonprofit agency serving death row inmates manage its mail and track its lawyers' pro bono hours. A journalism class teamed with a database systems class to help a nonprofit devoted to sustainability reporting improve its search functionality.[364]

Next semester, my data journalism students will partner with a local media outlet and a data visualization class to produce first-time voter guides through a community-centered journalism process that

363 Kim Pearson, Sarah Monisha Pulimood, Diane C Bates. Collaborating Across Boundaries to Engage Journalism Students in Computational Thinking, Teaching Journalism and Mass Communications, Winter, 2017 https://aejmc.us/spig/2017/collaborating-across-boundaries-to-engage-journalism-students-in-computational-thinking/
364 NSF Award #194869: Collaborating Across Boundaries to Engage Undergraduates in STEM Learning https://www.nsf.gov/awardsearch/showAward?AWD_ID=1914869

begins with understanding community information needs, priorities, and power dynamics. We are applying the same community-centered reporting approach to a current collaboration involving journalism, physics, public health, data visualization and environmental education classes in a project to improve neighborhood-level data and reporting on local urban heat islands. While these projects are works in progress, we have been able to identify ways in which colleges can provide the infrastructure to support best practices in these kinds of collaborations. [365]

There is still work to be done to connect this work back to pedagogy in data and computational journalism in explicit ways. Making those connects requires rethinking our how we train journalism educators to develop new epistemologies, ontologies and literacies, as I argued in In a 2021 blog post[366]. As we embark on that work, the principles that Dr. Gay articulated will doubtless continue to resonate as new generations of scholars take up her mantle. She and her colleagues have blazed the trail. It is up to all of us to build the transit network that will move all of our scholars to a more equitable future.

365 Kim Pearson, Sarah Monisha Pulimood, Diane C Bates. How Collaborating Across Boundaries Fosters Community-Engaged Partnerships, AAAS-IUSE blog July 25, 2022. https://www.aaas-iuse.org/how-collaborating-across-boundaries-fosters-community-engaged-partnerships/
366 Kim Pearson. What do 21st Century Journalism Educators Need to Know? KimPearson.net https://kimpearson.net/what-do-21st-century-journalism-educators-need-to-know/

# CHAPTER 10

# A Guide to Culturally Responsive Teaching: Educating Current and Future Engineers

*By Kelly J. Cross and Emily A. Affolter*

## Introduction

### Why is Culture Relevant to Engineering?

Although engineering has traditionally taken a position of colorblind meritocracy and that who you are as person does not matter, there are four reasons why culture is relevant to engineering: 1) a changing and increasingly diverse student population; 2) prior knowledge and schema need to bridge student learning; 3) student preparation for global engineering; and 4) the nature of engineering research is interdisciplinary.

To begin, we know that the deficit-based educational approaches have widely been adopted in engineering to fix systemically marginalized groups such as women, people of color, queer-identified, neuro-diverse, and students from lower SES to fit into the white male middle-class heterosexist dominant culture in engineering. Salazar explores deficit ideology's detrimental impacts on education regarding people of color, asserting that "Deficit notions of the resources of Communities of Color have fueled intolerance, bigotry, and assimilation throughout the history of U.S. public education."[367] As evidenced by years of historical and current data, these non-centered identities remain marginalized and underserved within engineering.[368] Although, the overall number of students enrolling in college have generally been on a steady incline, with the COVID-19 years being the exception, the growth was not matched with growth in the number of students from marginalized groups enrolled or graduating in STEM fields. As a result, the STEM disciplines have yet to modify their educational mission or teaching practices broadly to address the needs of a diverse student population. The problem of access to entry is further exacerbated through retention challenges once a student from a marginalized group enters a STEM discipline. Recent scholarship suggests that anyone but not everyone can be an engineer.[369] Also, engineers are socialized into developing an engineering identity and must be recognized by other engineers to be considered competent within the profession.[370] [371] [372] Given these facts, the culture of engineering is very relevant to increasing the participation of marginalized groups in the field and updating the teaching practices as an approach to make engineering more equitable.

In efforts to update the teaching practices in engineering we must consider what we know from basic learning theory, that we learn more efficiently when new information is connected to our prior

---

367 Maria Del Carmen Salazar, "A Humanizing Pedagogy: Reinventing the Principles and Practice of Education as a Journey Toward Liberation," Review of Research in Education 37, no.1 (2013): 122.
368 Joseph Roy, "Engineering by the numbers," American Society for Engineering Education, (2019):1-40.

369 Jacqueline Rohde, Derrick J. Satterfield, Miguel Rodriguez, Allison Godwin, Geoff Potvin, Lisa Benson, and Adam Kirn, "Anyone, But Not Everyone: Undergraduate Engineering Students' Claims of Who Can Do Engineering," Engineering Studies 12, no. 2 (2020): 82-103
370 K.L. Tonso, "Teams That Work: Campus Culture, Engineer Identity, and Social Interactions," Journal of Engineering Education 95 no. 1 (2006): 25-37.
371 K.L. Tonso, "Engineering Identity," in Cambridge Handbook of Engineering Education Research, eds. A. Johri & B. Olds (New York: Cambridge University Press, 2014), 267-282.
372 Allison Godwin, "The Development of a Measure of Engineering Identity" (paper presented at the American Society for Engineering Education Annual Conference & Exposition, New Orleans, 29 June 2016), https://monolith.asee.org/public/conferences/64/papers/14814/view

knowledge.[373] This is another key area where engineering has not been responsive to members of the field with non-centered identities. The colorblind approach[374] and hidden curriculum[375] within engineering has successfully limited the access to, entry and persistence in engineering but also minimized the rich cultural contributions people of color bring to the field. For example, the intentional exclusion of people of color from engineering[376] is often ignored if not outright dismissed by current engineers. Also, Lee[377] and other scholars [378]found that students of color experience racial microaggressions (RMAs) at all three levels (e.g., peers, faculty, campus climate), but Black students in the STEM majors are more likely to experience RMAs than other students of color. The predominantly white male faculty teaching in engineering has very little resources or motivation to connect the technical content in their course to the cultural background of students, especially students from marginalized groups. For example, some faculty see diversity as a policy and admissions issue,[379] where one engineering faculty commented, "As far as diversity goes, I have little control over that." Even national reports have pointed to this gap in the connection between faculty teaching and student learning[380]

373 Elia L. Congdon, Mee-Kyoung Kwon, and Susan C. Levine, "Learning to Measure through Action and Gesture: Children's Prior Knowledge Matters," Cognition, 180 (2018): 182–190. https://doi-org.prescottcollege.idm.oclc.org/10.1016/j.cognition.2018.07.002

374 Tabassum Fahim Ruby, "The American Dream, Colorblind Ideology, and Nationalism: Teaching Diversity Courses as a Woman Faculty of Color," Journal of Women and Gender in Higher Education 15, no. 2 (2022): 201–219, https://doi.org/10.1080/26379112.2022.2068023

375 Winston Kwame Abroampa, "The Hidden Curriculum and the Development of Latent Skills: The Praxis," Journal of Curriculum and Teaching 9, no. 2 (2020): 70–77.

376 Amy E. Slaton, Race, Rigor, and Selectivity in U.S. Engineering: The History of an Occupational Color Line, (Cambridge: Harvard University Press, 2010).

377 Meggan J. Lee, Jasmine D. Collins, Stacy Anne Harwood, Ruby Mendenhall, and Margaret Browne Huntt. ""If You Aren't White, Asian or Indian, You Aren't an Engineer": Racial Microaggressions in STEM Education," International Journal of STEM Education 7, no. 1 (2020): 1–16, doi:10.1186/s40594-020-00241-4.

378 Brea M. Banks and Steven E. Landau, "Cognitive Effects of Racial Microaggressions Directed at Black College Women," Journal of Negro Education 90, no. 1 (2021): 84–95.

379 Kelly J. Cross and Stephanie Cutler, "Engineering Faculty Perceptions of Diversity in the Classroom," (paper presented at the American Society of Engineering Education Annual Conference and Exposition, Columbus, Ohio, 25 - 28 June 2017), https://monolith.asee.org/public/conferences/78/papers/19343/view

380 Gary R. Howard, We Can't Teach What We Don't Know: White teachers, Multiracial Schools (New York: Teachers College Press, 2016).

Previous research revealed faculty as gate keepers to STEM fields and where faculty were unwilling to mentor students of color.[381] Other scholars noted how faculty of color experience being over scrutinized rather than acknowledged or celebrated for their contribution.[382] These examples demonstrate the devalued cultural contributions of people of color in STEM and highlight the lack of impetus to connect technical content to prior cultural knowledge students and faculty of color bring into the STEM classroom.

Another reason why culture is relevant to engineering is because the field is increasingly addressing complex global challenges that will require engineering students to confront global issues which have notable social contexts and societal implications. Reports by the National Academies of Engineering (NAE) including the Engineer of 2020 and calls from engineering education thought leaders specified globalization as a fact of life given the highly interdependent nature of our global society. Lohman defined global competence as "an ability to work knowledgeably and live comfortably in a transnational engineering environment and global society"[383] where engineering is needed to address worldwide issues like sustainability, human healthcare, and security. Concurrently, the National Academy for Engineering (NAE) released the Education the Engineer of 2020 along with a report that identified 14 grand challenges—both of which emphasized the interdependent nature of global problems that engineering would need to address.[384] More recently, the NAE released reports on the Challenges

381 McCoy, Dorian L., Courtney L. Luedke, and Rachelle Winkle-Wagner, "Encouraged or Weeded Out: Perspectives of Students of Color in the STEM Disciplines on Faculty Interactions," Journal of College Student Development 58, no. 5 (2017): 657-673.
382 Isis H. Settles, Martinque K. Jones, NiCole T. Buchanan, and Kristie Dotson, "Epistemic Exclusion: Scholar(Ly) Devaluation That Marginalizes Faculty of Color," Journal of Diversity in Higher Education 14, no. 4 (2021): 493–507, doi:10.1037/dhe0000174.
383 Jack R. Lohman, Howard A. Rollins, and J. Joseph Hoey, "Defining, Developing and Assessing Global Competence in Engineers," European Journal of Engineering Education 31, no.1 (2006): 119.
384 Charles M. Vest, "Educating Engineers for 2020 and Beyond," Reforming Engineering Education 36, no. 2 (2005): National Academy of Engineering (2005): 38-44.

of Engineering Education and Educating the Engineer 2030[385] [386] that stress the importance of the cultural context of engineering solutions for global issues. Finally, recent social medical phenomena like the COVID-19 virus illuminated the cultural context of global problems and the inequity that can be produced by ignoring the social context.[387] Therefore, these reports and realities stress engineers understanding the *cultural and social context* of problems, the problem-solving approach, and the proposed solution. In this piece, we offer culturally responsive teaching as a solution to educating current and future engineers on how culture is relevant (and vitally important) to our field.

The final evidence we present here that culture is relevant to engineering is the fact that the interdisciplinary nature of engineering research has become an essential practice. One scholar published an article in Nature that suggests interdisciplinary work can have broad societal and economic impacts that are not captured by citations.[388] Also, engineering education researchers found a difference in learning outcomes between interdisciplinary and single disciplinary majors.[389] Interestingly, STEM education scholars have proposed an interdisciplinary engineering education (IEE) curriculum. For example, a group of engineers claimed that an IEE curriculum is to train engineering students to bring together expertise from different disciplines in a single context and categorized IEE research within three focus areas: vision, teaching practices, and support.[390] Additionally, other

385 National Academies Press, Understanding the Educational and Career Pathways of Engineers (Washington DC: National Academies Press, 2018).
386 National Academies Press, Educating the Engineer of 2020: Adapting Engineering to the New Century (Washington DC: National Academies Press, 2005).
387 Kennedy B. Roberts, "African Americans and Covid-19: A Multifaceted Model of Biopsychosocial- Spiritual/Cultural Factors Addressing Disparities in Increased Covid-19 Infection," Journal of Cultural Diversity 28, no. 4 (2021): 88–97.
388 Richard Van Noorden, "Interdisciplinary Research by the Numbers," Nature 525 (2015): 306–307. https://doi.org/10.1038/525306a
389 Lisa R. Lattuca, David Knight, Tricia A. Seifert, Robert D. Reason, and Qin Liu, "Examining the Impact of Interdisciplinary Programs on Student Learning," Innovative Higher Education 42, no. 4 (2017): 337-353.
390 Antoine Van den Beemt, Miles MacLeod, Jan Van der Veen, Anne Van de Ven, Sophie van Baalen, Renate Klaassen, and Mieke Boon, "Interdisciplinary Engineering Education: A Review of Vision, Teaching, and Support," Journal of Engineering Education 109, no. 3 (2020): 508-555.

scholars call for updated assessment approaches for the student outcomes related to interdisciplinary knowledge.[391] Finally, recent STEM education reform has promoted the transformation from an individual-discipline-based education to an integrated STEM education and a new journal as a pioneering research journal dedicated to developing interdisciplinary research in STEM education as a distinct field.[392] As result, the recent developments from curriculum reform to novel research outlets demonstrate that the interdisciplinary characteristics of STEM education is growing and will continue to be intricately engrained into the STEM education and educational research.

## Culturally Responsive Teaching Principles

Dr. Geneva Gay's extensive collection of conceptual scholarship on culturally responsive teaching has significant reach with liberatory and just pedagogical and methodological implications for all domains of education. "Culturally responsive teaching can be defined as using the cultural knowledge, prior experiences, frames of reference, and performance styles of ethnically diverse students to make learning encounters more relevant to and effective for them. It teaches to and through the strengths of these students. Culturally responsive teaching is the behavioral expressions of knowledge, beliefs, and values that recognize the importance of racial and cultural diversity in learning." [393]Additionally, Gay describes cultural responsiveness as an educational methodology: "Culturally responsive teaching is a methodological arm of multicultural education, and part of that methodology... taught through their own cultural filters...If one ethnic group of students get the right to learn through the filters of their own cultural orientation, the argument of culturally responsive teaching is that

391Xiaoyi Gao, Peishan Li, Ji Shen, and Huifang Sun, "Reviewing Assessment of Student Learning in Interdisciplinary STEM Education," International Journal of STEM Education 7, no. 1 (2020): 1-14.

392 Yeping Li, "Promoting the Development of Interdisciplinary Research in STEM Education," Journal for STEM Education Research, 1 no. 1 (2018): 1-6.

393 Gay Geneva, Culturally Responsive Teaching: Theory, Research, and Practice (New York, Teachers College Press, 2018), 10.

other kids should have the same privileges."[394]

According to personal communication as a guest speaker in Affolter's "Culturally Responsive and Sustaining Pedagogies Course," Gay expressed that looking at multicultural education as a technical enterprise is a problem—and that "we should begin with why we are doing whatever we are doing... in order to teach human beings to be better at being human than they would be if we did not try to intervene in some way" Gay went on, asserting that "The essence of an educational endeavor is (or should be, at least in my mind) a humanizing process. Then the question becomes what does that mean?" She continues, "Whatever we do and however we do it, at the technical part of our interaction, is NOT to do injustice or indignity to the humanity or humanness of the people we are working with...There are ways in which we can engage in human interactions where dignity prevails regardless of our ideological, our political, our economic positions that we take."[395]

Geneva Gay, through her culturally responsive scholarship promotes honoring pluralistic identities in classrooms, and elevating (e.g., recognizing) the authenticity of every individual child. STEM disciplines have historically taught to specific norms that require assimilation. This assumes there is a "right" way to engage, a right way to speak, act, behave, and disseminate knowledge for STEM professionals, and often this singular approach erases cultural ways of being, knowing, and doing. For example, engineering education research has produced significant scholarship on students developing an engineering identity which consists of students identifying with the field but also being identified by others as an engineer. This will be discussed later in more detail in the implementation section. Culturally responsive teaching problematizes the singular dominant, hegemonic

---

394 Geneva Gay, interviewed by Valerie Kinloch, Ohio State University College of Education and Human Ecology, 2015. Retrieved from https://www.youtube.com/watch?v=MsyMbSiphTo
395 Geneva Gay, "Gay as Guest Speaker for Dr. Affolter's Prescott College Culturally Responsive and Sustaining Pedagogies PhD Course," Personal Communication, 2020. Retrieved from https://www.youtube.com/watch?v=MsyMbSiphTo

discourse, and challenges educators to think more pluralistically about every dimension of their teaching practice. According to Gay[396] there are five essential elements of culturally responsive teaching: 1) developing a knowledge base about cultural diversity, 2) including ethnic and cultural diversity content in the curriculum, 3) demonstrating caring and building learning communities, 4) communicating with ethnically diverse students, and 5) responding to ethnic diversity in instruction delivery. Here we provide a brief description of each component based on our understanding and within the context of engineering education:

- Cultural knowledge or competency is defined as educators developing the knowledge, skills, and abilities to create learning environments where students do not experience a conflict between their lived experience as STEM scholars and other parts of their identities.[397] The process of building cultural knowledge includes supporting students in developing a sense of belonging, by seeing themselves reflected in the environment, and their own beliefs and cultural practices being honored by STEM academic units that intentionally broaden accepted norms, practices, and ways of knowing. Gay recommends at a minimum, educators should be able to articulate the following: (a) which ethnic groups give priority to communal living and cooperative problem solving and how these preferences affect educational motivation, aspiration, and task performance; (b) how different ethnic groups' protocols of appropriate ways for children to interact with adults are exhibited in instructional settings; and (c) the implications of gender role socialization in different ethnic groups for implementing equity initiatives in

396 Geneva Gay, "Preparing for Culturally Responsive Teaching," Journal of Teacher Education 53, no. 2 (2002): 106-116.
397 Angela Johnson and Samantha Elliott, "Culturally Relevant Pedagogy: A Model to Guide Cultural Transformation in STEM Departments," Journal of Microbiology & Biology Education 21, no. 1 (2020):5.

classroom instruction.[398] These and additional reflective questions will be addressed in the "Critical Questioning Guide and Praxis" section.

- Related to cultural knowledge is the second tenet that requires educators to include ethnic and cultural diversity content in the curriculum. This component supports educators, especially engineering educators, to move beyond the null curriculum that only acknowledges contributions to engineering from the dominant discourse that privileges whiteness and seeks to discredit the contributions of STEM professionals that hold an identity as a member of a marginalized group.[399] An educator will have to intentionally include diverse representation within STEM technical content as it is not widely available currently.[400] For example, some scholars have called for an African-centered curriculum in STEM to illuminate the critical science-African culture connection.[401] Other scholars call for disrupting existing mainstream paradigms and practices in science education by liberating Black scholars with responsive education to foster the future of K-12 science teaching and learning that centers, embraces, and promotes historical and contemporary Black scientific innovation and creativity.[402]

398 Geneva Gay, "Preparing for Culturally Responsive Teaching," 107.

399 Brooke C. Coley, Denise R. Simmons, and Susan M. Lord, "Dissolving the Margins: LEANING IN to an Antiracist Review Process," Journal of Engineering Education 110, no. 1 (2021): 8-14.

400 Catherine L. Quinlan, "Emergent Themes and Pragmatic Research Methods for Meaningful Cultural Representation of Blacks in Multimedia Products for the Science Classroom," International Journal of Science Education 43, no. 14 (2021): 2316-2332, DOI: 10.1080/09500693.2021.1959959.

401 Samuel M. Burbanks, Kmt G. Shockley, and Kofi LeNiles, "The Need for African Centered Education in STEM Programs for Black Youth," Journal of African American Males in Education 11, no. 2 (2020): 12-24.

402 Terrell R. Morton, Monica L. Miles, ReAnna S. Roby, and Nickolaus A. Ortiz, "All We Wanna Do Is Be Free": Advocating for Black Liberation in and through K-12 Science Education," Journal of Science Teacher Education 33, no. 2 (2022): 131-153, DOI: 10.1080/1046560X.2021.2008096.

- Taking an interest in the diverse students that may be in your classroom and including diverse representation (that mirrors them) in the curriculum, are first steps to demonstrate caring and establishing learning communities. For STEM educators, recall that caring is a key component of motivation theories widely used in engineering education research.[403] In this article, the authors show how STEM student motivation and choices are impacted by their perceptions of being cared about and valued within their academic environment. More recently, McGee demonstrated how the lack of caring negatively impacts Black students in STEM.[404] Also, establishing learning communities is consistent with common pedagogical tools used in STEM education including cooperative learning[405] and team-based learning[406] [407] Establishing a responsive learning community requires STEM educators to apply student-centered approaches to their teaching and optimizing student engagement as a "guide on the side" rather than a "sage on the stage."

- An essential step in establishing a welcoming learning community for diverse students is finding ways to effectively communicate with students who are ethnically diverse.

403 Brett D. Jones, Marie C. Paretti, Serge F. Hein, and Tamara W. Knott, "An Analysis of Motivation Constructs with First-Year Engineering Students: Relationships Among Expectancies, Values, Achievement, and Career Plans," Journal of Engineering Education 99, no. 4 (2010): 319-336.

404 Ebony McGee, "Fear, Fuel, and Fire!: Black STEM Doctoral Students' Career Decisions during the Trump Presidency," International Journal of Qualitative Studies in Education (2021): 1-21, DOI: 10.1080/09518398.2021.1930246

405 Karl A. Smith, "Cooperative Learning: Effective Teamwork for Engineering Classrooms," (paper presented at the Frontiers in Education 25th Annual Conference, Atlanta, Georgia, November, 1995), file:///C:/Users/a136096/Downloads/Smith-CL-Eng_Classes-IEEE-1995.pdf

406 Homero Gregorio Murzi, "Team-Based Learning Theory Applied to Engineering Education: A Systematic Review of Literature," (paper presented at the American Society for Engineering Education Annual Conference & Exposition, Indianapolis, Indiana, June 2014), https://monolith.asee.org/public/conferences/32/papers/10751/view

407 Maria Parappilly, Richard John Woodman, and Sharmil Randhawa, "Feasibility and Effectiveness of Different Models of Team-Based Learning Approaches in STEMM-Based Disciplines," Research in Science Education 51, no. 1 (2021): 391-405.

As we know, education is a social event, predicated on the ability to be heard and understood. Effective communication requires STEM educators to hear the voice of students who are diverse although (and in fact, in part, because) it may be verbiage and verse that is not part of mainstream hegemonic discourse. As a result, a responsive approach to effective communication that disrupts white supremacy is to broaden our definitions of what "is" acceptable scholarly communication. Additionally, some Black scholars suggest that African Americans have been cut off from their native language and culture which can limit our own understanding of the Black lived experience because we did not have the language to explain.[408] Therefore, educators will have to engage in the ongoing process of developing open and effective lines of communication with students who are diverse with diverse standards of communication styles and preferences.

- Establishing effective communication with diverse students can be manifested in the final component, responding to ethnic diversity in instruction delivery. Varying instructional delivery requires preparation and effort on the part of educators to step out of their comfort zone of their preferred teaching style, especially in STEM. The traditional method of direct lecturing still dominates STEM education teaching despite decades of research showing improved student learning with active and engagement strategies. Thus, this component of responsive teaching will require a paradigm shift of STEM educators and a willingness to at least try to implement research-based teaching practices or RBIS. Keeping in mind that culturally responsive teaching

---

408 Malidoma Patrice Somé, Of Water and the Spirit: Ritual, Magic, and Initiation in the Life of an African Shaman (New York: Penguin, 1995).

is a research-based pedagogy, it just has not been widely adopted within the STEM classroom. Finally, we would encourage STEM educators to consider varying the corresponding assessment approach as they execute varying types of instructional delivery. The assessment should match the delivery and accurately measure the desired learning outcomes.

## Culturally Responsive Teaching Critical Questioning Guide and Praxis

Some scholars have cultivated tools to make culturally responsive teaching more accessible to more higher education faculty and one example is the work of author two (Emily A. Affolter) and her colleague Sarah Rosman. After countless teachers, instructional coaches, district leaders and faculty members asked for a culturally responsive toolkit, they developed a few key questions to help guide educators towards making more informed and reflexive decisions in the classroom. The Culturally Responsive Teaching Critical Questioning Guide is not meant to be a checklist, or a one-size-fits-all approach to contemplative culturally responsive teaching. Instead, it is a starting point for educators to begin to build the habit of mind to ask questions that unpack hegemonic assumptions about their practice, and begin to invite more just, liberatory, humane, and equitable approaches to curriculum development. It is a primer to thinking, behaving, acting, and teaching in ways that disrupt status quo teaching and invite sustaining pedagogies that cultivate belonging for all students.

## Culturally Responsive Critical Questioning Guide
- What underlying assumptions or values are embedded in this curriculum/lesson?

- Is this content universally applicable, or would it be more beneficial for some than others? For whom and in what circumstances?

- What people/groups may be left out of the conversation? To whom does this content apply? In what circumstances? Why? Who might this content exclude? In what circumstances? Why?

- How do you relate to this lesson? How does that inform your read and delivery of it?

  - Is this content that was taught in your home growing up? In your school as a student? As a teacher? Consider your relationship to this lesson based on your history and socialization with it.

  - How might your own history with a lesson/content or related knowledge inform your teaching of it?

- How have you seen this content represented in the public sphere? By whom? In what ways? For what purposes?

- Does the appropriateness of this lesson change from context to context? If so, how? If this is the case, in what ways do you make this explicit with students?

  - In what circumstances could this content be teaching positive archetypes/ideals?

  - In what circumstances could this content be teaching negative or harmful archetypes/ideals?

  - How might you articulate this to your students?

- What is the intended purpose of this curriculum? What might it look like to be successful with this content?

  - What kinds of questions could you ask your students to

draw out the impact it has on them, as well as wonderings, aversions, and critiques of the curriculum?

- What are the intended products (i.e. oral presentation, poster, essay, skit, storyline character & setting, etc.) produced for the end of this unit, and how does that influence the delivery of content? Does the product, in fact, enhance what you are doing and if so, how? Does it contribute to deeper understanding of the topic? How do you know?

- What other questions would further hold you accountable to equitable ideals in your curriculum-refining process?

Praxis can be defined as the commitment to practice that involves constant reflection, and the reflection informs one's subsequent action. The concept of praxis has direct theoretical relevance to critical pedagogy and culturally responsive teaching. Freire explained that the discovery of oppressive conditions "cannot be purely intellectual but must involve action; nor can it be limited to mere activism but must include serious reflection: only then will it be a praxis."[409] When applied to teaching, praxis requires teachers to alter traditional norms of teaching and learning.

Fernández further unpacks the implications of the praxis process for educators: "Restoring our humanity is a political process as well as an act of love and, in the context of professional development, can only take place if there is a commitment to revolutionary praxis."[410] Also, Villanueva would argue that moving toward a socially just pedagogical praxis requires "teaching as an instinctual craft"[411] that was centered on decolonial reflection and action, involving the negation of standardized pedagogical practice, and embracing "critically con-

409 Paulo Freire, Pedagogy of the Oppressed (New York: Continuum, 1970), 52.
410 Anita E. Fernández, "Decolonizing Professional Development: A Re-humanizing Approach," Equity & Excellence in Education 52, no. 2/3 (2019): 188, https://doi.org/10.1080/106 65684.2019.1649610
411 Silvia Toscano Villanueva, "Teaching as a Healing Craft: Decolonizing the Classroom and Creating Spaces of Hopeful Resistance through Chicano-Indigenous Pedagogical Praxis," The Urban Review 45, no. 1 (2013): 29, doi:10.1007/s11256- 012-0222-5

scious, socially just pedagogical praxis."[412] They go on to describe some of their student engagement that involved course "readings, assignments, class discussions, field trips, and community intellectuals in [their] classes have gone on to challenge the coloniality of power and incessant proliferation of racial hierarchy and gender inequality existing in the world."[413] All of this, for Villanueva, came from their teaching instincts, "And [they] have chosen to listen."[414]

## Adoption and Implementation Considerations

In this section, we will highlight considerations for adopting culturally responsive teaching in STEM classrooms. The considerations include: 1) teacher authenticity; 2) managing personal bias; 3) acknowledging student multiple identities and 4) simple tips for inclusive teaching practices. Teacher authenticity is defined as an educator delivering instructional communication in a manner that is consistent with their overall sense of self and a person-centered approach to teacher–student communication.[415] So being self-aware of (understanding and bringing a willingness to unpack) your personal values regarding education is a key to implementing culturally responsive teaching. Articulating your values for the purpose of being transparent with students, can foster you having authentic communication with diverse students. Similarly, acknowledging your personal bias is another key step for instructors to adopt culturally responsive teaching into their teaching practices.[416] Personal bias is defined as prejudice in favor of or against one thing, person, or group compared with another, or uncritically accepting conclusions that fit with our personal experience or beliefs that unconsciously influences our

---

412 Ibid.
413 Ibid.
414 Ibid.
415 Zac D. Johnson and Sara LaBelle, "An Examination of Teacher Authenticity in the College Classroom," Communication Education 66, no. 4 (2017): 423-439, DOI: 10.1080/03634523.2017.1324167.
416 Patricia Clark and Eva Zygmunt, "A Close Encounter with Personal Bias: Pedagogical Implications for Teacher Education," The Journal of Negro Education 83, no. 2 (2014): 147-161.

decision making.[417] Personal bias has been a persistent and invisible problem in STEM[418] [419] [420] Educators should find ways to regularly monitor their personal bias including utilizing the Implicit Attitude test and also checking in with colleagues about how they perceive attitudes and student interactions. Acknowledging personal bias supports faculty-student interactions which also requires that STEM faculty recognize that all students bring their multiple identities into the classroom. Students' multiple and intersecting identities impact how they experience their engineering education.[421] [422] [423] Thus, instructional and assessment variation are effective ways to allow students to demonstrate mastery of knowledge within the context of their multiple identities, offering multiple pathways to success. Finally, instructional variation and equitable assessments are part of inclusive teaching practices. STEM educators can apply various levels of inclusive teaching practices from adding a diversity statement to their syllabus to designing an entire course or curriculum around culturally responsive teaching principles. Keeping in mind that the different inclusive

417 B. Keith Payne, Heidi A. Vuletich and Kristjen B. Lundberg, "The Bias of Crowds: How Implicit Bias Bridges Personal and Systemic Prejudice," Psychological Inquiry 28 no. 4 (2017): 233-248, DOI:10.1080/1047840X.2017.1335568.

418 Corinne A. Moss-Racusin, Aneta K. Molenda, and Charlotte R. Cramer, "Can Evidence Impact Attitudes? Public Reactions to Evidence of Gender Bias in STEM Fields," Psychology of Women Quarterly 39, no. 2 (2015): 194-209.

419 Ebony O. McGee, "Devalued Black and Latino Racial Identities: A By-Product of STEM College Culture?" American Educational Research Journal 53, no. 6 (2016): 1626-1662.

420 Tess L. Killpack and Laverne C. Melón, "Toward Inclusive STEM Classrooms: What Personal Role Do Faculty Play?" CBE—Life Sciences Education 15, no. 3 (2016): es3.

421 Kelly J. Cross and Marie C. Paretti, "Identification with Academics and Multiple Identities: Combining Theoretical Frameworks to Better Understand the Experiences of Minority Engineering Students," (paper presented at the American Society for Engineering Education Annual Conference & Exposition, San Antonio, Texas, June 2012), https://monolith.asee.org/public/conferences/8/papers/4060/view

422 Adam Kirn, Allison Godwin, Lisa Benson, Geoff Potvin, Jacqueline Doyle, Hank Boone, and Dina Verdin, "Intersectionality of Non-Normative Identities in the Cultures of Engineering," (paper presented at the American Society for Engineering Education Annual Conference & Exposition, New Orleans, Louisiana, June 2016), https://peer.asee.org/intersectionality-of-non-normative-identities-in-the-cultures-of-engineering

423 Kelly J. Cross, Kathryn Clancy, Ruby Mendenhall, Princess Imoukhuede, and Jennifer R. Amos, "The Double Bind of Race and Gender: A Look into the Experiences of Women of Color in Engineering," (paper presented at American Society of Engineering Education Annual Conference & Exposition, Columbus, Ohio, 24-28 June 2017), file:///C:/Users/a136096/Downloads/the-double-bind-of-race-and-gender-a-look-into-the-experiences-of-women-of-color-in-engineering1.pdf

teaching practices may require varying amounts of effort on the part of the educator including engaging with scholarship of teaching and learning (SOTL) research based instructional strategies (RBIS's) and collaborating a local campus teaching and learning center.

**Culturally Responsive Teaching in the STEM classroom**

This chapter began with a broad orientation to culturally responsive pedagogical foundations across educational realms, and this subsequent section focuses on how the authors have operationalized these principles in their STEM classrooms. With a culturally responsive pedagogical foundation, we offer examples of how one might apply these concepts in practice. These examples illustrate the process of engaging with culturally responsive teaching as an active choice and constant learning, rather than a point of arrival, so please read these as an invitation to engage, wonder, and practice accordingly (rather than a linear road map). These STEM methodological orientations are grounded in our culturally responsive teaching philosophy rooted in a humanizing pedagogy, a pedagogy of love, and an emphasis on students' wellbeing above all.

STEM education specifically needs attention, relentlessly claiming equity pedagogy and striving for liberation. Many STEM faculty members tend to be hired "for their disciplinary credentials"[424] in lieu of experience teaching, student-centered approach, and commitments to advancing equity. "Despite significant efforts to broaden participation in postsecondary science, technology, engineering, and math (STEM) education, students from historically minoritized populations continue to face systemic barriers related to access, departmental climate, and institutional practices."[425] Both significant academic sup-

424 Cheryl D. Ching and Maxine T. Roberts, "Crafting a Racial Equity Practice in College Math Education," Journal of Diversity in Higher Education 15, no. 4 (2022): 402. EBSCOhost, https://doi.org/10.1037/dhe0000379

425 Brian A. Burt, Blayne D. Stone, Rudisang Motshubi, Lorenzo D. Baber, "STEM Validation among Underrepresented Students: Leveraging Insights from a STEM Diversity Program to Broaden Participation," Journal of Diversity in Higher Education (2020): 1 Advance Online Publication. https://doi.org/10.1037/dhe0000300.

port through mentorship, and an evolving emphasis on systemically minoritized students in STEM's scientific and identity development were culturally responsive practices informing Burt et al.'s study.

Additionally, it is also important to note that the COVID-19 pandemic has affected those with systemically minoritized identities in STEM adversely in the educational sector. For example, according to Hun Kyoung Ro et al. "Women have been underrepresented in STEM in the past, and we worry that the pandemic's social and economic impact is disproportionately affecting women and could disrupt progress toward gender equity in STEM."[426] Culturally responsive teaching must be adapted contextually and stay nimble, taking stock of and understanding the conditions that people are living through in order to appropriately offer instruction that honors the range of human experience.

Employing explicit STEM Equity Pedagogy, there are a number of ways we have operationalized culturally responsive pedagogies in our own classrooms. In order to bring this theory to practice, there is a critical undercurrent of teacher transformative self-study that needs to take place. This involves, at core, that faculty "understand why race [and equity] must be centered in math [and STEM] reform and how traditional ways of teaching impact Black and Latinx/a/o students."[427] Awareness of one's (the educator's) own participation in systems of oppression, and knowledge about the material inequities in STEM, coupled with a reflexive attitude that requires iterative curiosity are foundational to operationalizing culturally responsive content. Centered in the teaching mathematics discipline, Ching and Roberts assert that "racial equity demands a race conscious approach that (a) presses faculty to make sense of who they are, what they believe, and how they teach" in addition to "(b)uncovers the norms and logics of math education" and finally, "advances a humanizing pedagogy in

426 Ro, Hyun Kyoung, Elizabeth J. Ramon, and Frank Fernandez, Gender Equity in STEM in Higher Education (Oxfordshire: Taylor and Francis, 2021), 8.
427 Ching, Cheryl D., and Maxine T. Roberts. "Crafting a Racial Equity Practice in College Math Education." 401.

which minoritized students feel validated and cared for as learners and persons with complex lives."[428]

Committed to teacher transformative self-study, we, the authors, engage in continuous critical dialogue, reflection, and learning that helps us clarify and crystallize our own understandings of systemic oppression, how we might be complicit with those systems, and what we can do on both micro and meta scales to interrupt and interrogate the hegemony. This looks like focused reading and studying from systemically minoritized and liberatory thinkers, honest and vulnerable conversations with our colleagues and friends, facilitating and engaging in racial affinity groups, and remaining curious, accountable, and humble. With that backdrop, we will highlight our own pedagogical examples or cases from the STEM higher education classroom that showcase 1) syllabus building and changes, 2) equitable teamwork, 3) feedback solicitation and integration, 4) assessment, and 5) community building. All of these examples feature student-centrism and an innate curiosity about how students' own selves as cultural, pluralistic beings, can be reflected in the course material and experience.

In a culturally responsive classroom, a course syllabus is a living, emergent document. We have built our syllabi with both pre-existing content and objectives, but also a bent towards emergence. This also draws upon Adrienne Maree Brown's work, describing emergent strategy: "Change is constant. (Be like water)....Move at the speed of trust. Focus on critical connections more than critical mass—build the resilience by building the relationships. Less prep, more presence, what you pay attention to grows."[429] One culturally unresponsive misunderstanding of a course syllabus is that it is static.

Roughly half of what we integrate in a syllabus is pre-planned and pre-existing, but a significant amount of a course needs to emerge with the group. When students begin a class, we find ways to solicit

---

428 Ibid, 401-402.
429 Adrienne Maree Brown, Emergent Strategy: Shaping Change, Changing Worlds (Chico: AK Press, 2017), 41-42.

meaning from them, posing questions (through 1:1 meetings, or introductory assignments/discussions) such as: Why is this class meaningful to you? What knowledge and/or experience are you bringing with you that will inform your understanding of it? What skills do you seek to leave with and why? What do we (the instructors and your peers) need to know about you in order to work together, and why?

It may be that a student has their own podcast and could use it as a platform for a signature assignment, or another student might have a family member that works in a related STEM field that could host an optional webinar to showcase the relevance of their skills. One student might be preparing for a specific job that the course could help bolster more discrete skills for their CV. Getting to know the students individually, and their own personal goals and schema for the content is simply good culturally responsive teaching.

Also, the syllabus can shift and live with intentional adaptation. As Adrienne Maree Brown reflects, "Adaptation reduces exhaustion. No one bears the burden alone of figuring out the next move and muscling toward it. There is an efficiency at play—is something not working? Stop. Change. If something is working, keep doing it—learning and innovating as you go."[430] The COVID-19 pandemic, for example, continues to teach us lessons about what stressors our students are experiencing, and how much burnout and overwhelm (in addition to grief, illness, and loss) many are living with. The zoom fatigue can accumulate over the series of a course. We continuously assess our learning community and check to see if due dates for assignments need to shift, meeting times might need to be condensed or made asynchronous, and even if group work needs to become individual to meet personal needs and mitigate stressors.

Also, teamwork is commonly employed in the STEM classroom, and working across ideological and human difference can be highly culturally responsive, but must be scaffolded appropriately, as without

---

430 Ibid, 71.

proper planning, teamwork often results in reinforcing inequities.[431] Most often, when we assign students to work in teams/labs without scaffolding, students with the most systemically minoritized identities tend to do extra background work, like notetaking or documenting results. When the team is asked to present their work, usually students with more dominant/privileged identities tend to take credit for the work, like speaking about their results on behalf of the class. Quinn et al. researched physics labs in educational settings and found: "the importance of structuring equitable group dynamics in educational settings, as a gendered division of roles can emerge without active intervention" encouraging STEM instructors to not only "remove explicitly biased aspects of curricula but also take active steps to ensure that potentially discriminatory aspects are not inadvertently reinforced."[432]

STEM instructors should equitably scaffold class teams, identify role assignments and specific student tasks early, and ensure all roles rotate so all students can participate in all roles.[433] For example, you might have 1) a spokesperson, 2) a notetaker, and 3) a timekeeper. Be explicit about the function of these roles and make sure that each student is participating equally in each role so all experience the range of outcomes rather than fall into patterns that reinforce who feels they have voice (or who feels inadvertently silenced) in the classroom.

Another culturally responsive teaching strategy for STEM learners is soliciting students' feedback continuously in the classroom, and letting students know that you received it, and if/how you will act on it. Building a constant platform (which the authors have done weekly or bi-weekly in an online personal forum) that encourages students

431 Vereen G. Linwood, Clewiston D. Challenger, Nicole R. Hill, Vaibhavee R. Agaskar, and Jean Georgiou, "I Did My Part: Responding to Inequitable Group Project Contributions," in Critical Incidents in Counselor Education: Teaching, Supervision, Scholarship, Leadership, and Advocacy, ed. Jacqueline M. Swank and Casey A. Barrio Minton (American Counseling Association, 2022), 13–20.
432 Katherine N. Quinn, Michelle M. Kelly, Kathryn L. McGill, Emily M. Smith, Zachary Whipps, and N.G. Holmes, "Group Roles in Unstructured Labs Show Inequitable Gender Divide," Physical Review Physics Education Research 16 no.1 (2020): 1.
433 Ibid, 11.

to reflect how the course is going for them and what they might do to improve upon it for that particular student's experience is critical. Equally important is to indicate there are no negative consequences to students' feedback. I (author Emily Affolter) have had remarkable success with this experience. When teaching a doctoral level sustainability course, one student (a person of color) felt there were too many resources critically examining white privilege/white supremacy culture and wished for more resources that focused on person-of-color liberation work. That was such important feedback, and I received it with gratitude, acted immediately to build a parallel repository of resources that focused on systemically minoritized/impacted communities' liberation, and since then, the resources that I added (in a timely manner) will be part of the course as it lives on into the future. There are also times that student feedback can not be integrated or applied, at least in a timely way, and the responsive act would be to acknowledge their feedback quickly, and also address the why behind not immediately integrating it (like resource limitations, or timeline, etc.). In a culturally responsive classroom, all students' voices matter, and need to be sought out to inform a deliberately student-centric learning environment.

Culturally responsive assessment requires ways to address "unique learning needs of diverse student populations" and assessment, as it stands, without an equitable orientation.[434] Culturally responsive assessment "privileges and validates certain types of learning and evidence of learning over others, can hinder the validation of multiple means of demonstration, and can reinforce within students the false notion that they do not belong in higher education."[435] Assessment can either reinforce inequities, or it can be a pathway for students to feel seen and recognized for their assets and hard work. For Inuit children,

---

434 Erick Montenegro and Natasha A. Jankowski, "Equity and Assessment: Moving towards Culturally Responsive Assessment," National Institute for Learning Outcomes Assessment January (2017): 1-23, https://www.learningoutcomesassessment.org/wp-content/uploads/2019/02/OccasionalPaper29.pdf

435 Ibid, 5.

for example, assessment practices that are "Eurocentrically biased assessment practices is demotivation toward school which results in a decline in school attendance, which adds additional challenges for school success."[436] In Inukitut, the culturally responsive assessment program has been described as *Sivuniksamut Ilinniarniq* (SI), and SI both "promotes mastery and developing expertise,"[437] which are both characteristics of high value in Inuit society.

Questions about assessment we ask ourselves as STEM educators are: how can assessment be formative (continuous and low stakes), rather than simply summative/singular? How might we provide feedback to our students over time (recognizing their arcs of growth and effort) that has equal or more value than a singular final product? This could look like coaching students through a long project and evaluating the energy and effort they continuously exhibited and weighing that effort significantly towards a final grade. How might we de-center ourselves as educators and invite the students to self-assess, or assess their peers (to leverage and honor their own feedback as worthy and valid)? How might we invite our students into building assessment processes with us, such that the metrics of assessment align with the skills the students seek to bring? How might we invite students' own funds of knowledge and cultural assets into assignments so they can utilize their preexisting talents to communicate what they have learned?

Finally, culturally responsive teaching in the STEM classroom needs to center relationships and cultivate opportunities for more-than-content oriented connections. For example, in the current Decolonizing Research in East Africa course that author Emily Affolter is currently teaching, she and her co-instructor provided two-hour-sessions every other week with no agenda or content goals and invited students to attend them. While content invariably would

---

436 Kathy Snow, Tess Miller, and Melanie O'Gorman, "Strategies for Culturally Responsive Assessment Adopted by Educators in Inuit Nunangat," Diaspora, Indigenous, and Minority Education 15, no. 1 (2021): 63.
437 Ibid., 64.

come up, as this was an intrinsically motivated group, these optional meetings often ended up with 100% student attendance and were centered on connection and relationship building. In Bell's research, "approachability, empathy, and staff-student interactions were strong predictors of student satisfaction" [438]and this increases the sense of belonging for all students in the course, particular students with more minoritized identities.

As Howson et al.'s research on belonging in science reveals, "For students, a sense of belonging may represent feelings of acceptance and connection. Indeed, students' sense of belonging is known to be strongly associated with wellbeing, academic achievement, and a successful life at university."[439] Building a STEM learning community of belonging can simply involve opening up space and access to the educator/faculty member that is not associated with the course content, and inviting students to bring their whole selves in. This could also look like a picnic, or a zoom "coffee" or even building a Jamboard or online platform for people to express themselves beyond the confines of the course content.

The examples we drew upon, exploring dimensions of teacher transformative self-study and student-centered learning in the STEM classroom, and digging into the following realms: showcase 1) syllabus building and changes, 2) equitable teamwork, 3) feedback solicitation and integration, 4) assessment, and 5) community building, are simply a starting point. There are countless ways to operationalize culturally responsive teaching in the STEM classroom, and no singular or "right" approach. The key is to commit to a responsive classroom, adapt it to the students themselves, and involve/inquire/include them every step of the way, so they not only feel centered and that they belong, but that their voices so respected they are critically informing the teaching itself.

438 Karen Bell, "Increasing Undergraduate Student Satisfaction in Higher Education: The Importance of Relational Pedagogy," Journal of Further & Higher Education 46, no. 4 (2022): 492.
439 Camille Kandiko Howson, Ian M. Kinchin, and Karen Gravett. "Belonging in Science: Democratic Pedagogies for Cross-Cultural PhD Supervision," Education Sciences 12, no. 2 (2022): 121.

## Conclusions

In conclusion, there are three/four main takeaways from this chapter:

- STEM false narrative of meritocracy has allowed little progress towards diversity, equity and inclusion (DEI) outcomes, we provided multiple examples of how culture is relevant to engineering and STEM more broadly.

- Some STEM education scholars have suggested the core principles of culturally responsive teaching are the pathway to update STEM teaching practices.

- Next we provided a tool with critical questions to guide STEM educators to consider culturally responsive teaching in their instruction and we lay the foundation for reflection and informed and critically conscious praxis to engage in constant improvement of teaching for an increasingly diverse student body.

- We close with specific strategies and considerations for implementing culturally responsive teaching into the STEM culture and teaching including teacher authenticity.

- Overall, we wrote this chapter to be a guide for STEM faculty to navigate implementing culturally responsive teaching into their instructional practices.

Apprentice House is the country's only campus-based, student-staffed book publishing company. Directed by professors and industry professionals, it is a nonprofit activity of the Communication Department at Loyola University Maryland.

Using state-of-the-art technology and an experiential learning model of education, Apprentice House publishes books in untraditional ways. This dual responsibility as publishers and educators creates an unprecedented collaborative environment among faculty and students, while teaching tomorrow's editors, designers, and marketers.

Outside of class, progress on book projects is carried forth by the AH Book Publishing Club, a co-curricular campus organization supported by Loyola University Maryland's Office of Student Activities.

Eclectic and provocative, Apprentice House titles intend to entertain as well as spark dialogue on a variety of topics. Financial contributions to sustain the press's work are welcomed. Contributions are tax deductible to the fullest extent allowed by the IRS.

To learn more about Apprentice House books or to obtain submission guidelines, please visit www.apprenticehouse.com.

Apprentice House
Communication Department
Loyola University Maryland
4501 N. Charles Street
Baltimore, MD 21210
Ph: 410-617-5265 • Fax: 410-617-2198
info@apprenticehouse.com • www.apprenticehouse.com